D0912683

Truly Fed

finding freedom from disordered eating

Gari Meacham

BEACON HILL PRESS
OF KANSAS CITY

Copyright 2009
by Gari Meacham and Beacon Hill Press of Kansas City

ISBN 978-0-8341-2464-6

Printed in the
United States of America

Cover Design: Brandon Hill
Inside Design: Sharon Page

Library of Congress Cataloging-in-Publication Data

Meacham, Gari.
  Truly fed : finding freedom from disordered eating / Gari Meacham.
    p. cm.
  Includes bibliographical references.
  ISBN 978-0-8341-2464-6 (pbk.)
  1. Spiritual healing. 2. Eating disorders—Religious aspects—Christianity.
3. Food—Religious aspects—Christianity. 4. Dinners and dining—Religious aspects—Christianity. I. Title.
  BT732.5.M435 2009
  248.4—dc22

                                         2009018227

10 9 8 7 6 5 4 3 2 1

Truly Fed

CONTENTS

Acknowledgments   7

Introduction   9

1. Are You Ready to Get Well?   11

2. An Honest Look at What's Eating You   29

3. What Are You Really Hungry For?   53

4. Do You Dare Eat What Is Set Before You?   81

5. That Was Then—This Is Now   93

6. Whose Voice Is That?   117

7. The Pleasing Texture of Freedom and Success   137

8. Sanity for the Long Haul   155

A Note from the Author   169

Appendix   171

  Disordered Eating Through the Eyes of
  Your Loved Ones   173

  Raising Children to Have a Healthy Relationship
  with Food   177

  Dieting Isn't the Answer   181

  Real Stories from Real Women   183

Notes   187

ACKNOWLEDGMENTS

I once heard an author say that to write a book is to puncture a vein and draw your own blood. I agree with that sentiment! Through the pages of this text flow my blood, sweat, and tears. It's been a labor of love twenty years in the making.

As in any endeavor worthy of our time and tears, there are many people I would like to thank:

- My husband, Bobby, who never quit rooting me on to complete this work. His words, prayers, and power talks pushed me to believe it was possible.
- My three children—Brooke, Ally, and Colton. You are my treasure and my crown. The love and respect I feel for you can't be captured in words.
- My mom, dad, sister, and brother—who model courage and tenacity each day of their lives.
- My friends and "Upper Room Prayer Gals" who have sat before God with me, inquiring and listening for direction with *Truly Fed*.
- My greatest thanks is offered to Jesus, the author and perfecter of my faith. It is only through Him that I have the joy of healing and the grace to share about it.

INTRODUCTION
INVITATION TO THE READER

Welcome to *Truly Fed*. As you begin this journey, I would like to clarify a few things for you before we move into the text:

- I purposely use the term *disordered eating* rather than *eating disorder*. When we think of eating disorders, we tend to think of those thin anorexics or treatment center graduates, forgetting that yo-yo dieting, compulsive overeating, and a body image badgered by self-doubt also fall into the category of *disorder*. By simply exchanging the order of the words, I hope to bring a different light to a term that's often misunderstood.

- Throughout the book I reference many scriptures that are powerful in the healing of disorder. Some ladies gave me a sign that says, "A messed-up Bible belongs to someone who is not!" I hope you *mess up* your Bible with sticky notes and highlighting as you work through this text.

- As you read through *Truly Fed*, you'll notice that I look at food-related issues through three lenses: those of the overeater, the anorexic, and the bulimic. You may relate to one area more than another, but often we find ourselves struggling with areas that overlap.

Yours on the journey,
Gari

ONE

Are You Ready to Get Well?

While standing in my closet looking at clothes that were either too small for me or that I was terrified to try on, one thing became clear: I had to get well whatever the cost. For years I had straddled the "healing fence," with one foot reaching for the ground of wholeness and mental sanity regarding food, while the rest of my body clung to the fence of cherished habits and defeated thinking. Countless women have sorrowfully said to me, "I want to get well—I just don't know what it takes to get there!" Isn't it interesting that the very thing that paralyzes our lives becomes something we hang on to and refuse to change?

Regular overeating, secret binges, throwing-up rituals, and perpetual dieting all languish in the realm of heartache, yet we resist letting go of these behaviors.

Long ago I heard a story about a man who struggled with a life of addiction and defeat. When he was confronted about his life, the man's shocking response was "I may live in hell, but at least I know all the street names!"

Isn't this how a life plagued by disordered eating looks? We know it's a hellish prison, but we're used to the scenery. Some habits and twisted ways of thinking have become so familiar that living differently seems impossible.

In John 5 Jesus encounters a "hell dweller." The man in this scripture had struggled for 38 years with an infirmity of some kind. We can infer that he couldn't walk, but he also struggled with emotional paralysis that was just as damaging.

> Soon another feast came around and Jesus was back in Jerusalem. Near the Sheep Gate in Jerusalem there was a pool, in Hebrew called Bethesda, with five alcoves. Hundreds of sick people—blind, crippled, paralyzed—were in these alcoves. One man had been an invalid there for thirty-eight years. When Jesus saw him stretched out by

the pool, and knew how long he had been there, He asked "Do you want to get well?"

The sick man said, "Sir, when the water is stirred, I don't have anybody to put me in the pool. By the time I get there, somebody else is already in."

Jesus said "Get up, take your bedroll, and start walking." The man was healed on the spot. He picked up his bedroll and walked off *(John 5:1-9, TM)*.

Jesus saw this man lying in an alcove, crumbled on his bedroll. He *knew* he had been in this state a long time, and without any small talk or meaningless conversation, He probed to the very soul of the man by asking "Do you want to get well?"

When I read this scripture for the first time, I was tempted to use a phrase my kids used to chant when they were young teenagers: "Duh!" *Of course* he wanted to get well! Why else would he lie there for years with the vague hope of crawling into the pool and getting healed? It struck me that Jesus deliberately asked him this searing question. He made the man face where he was physically and emotionally in his infirmity. The man bombarded Jesus with reasons he couldn't help himself. "Sir, I don't have any help. I'm trying to do this all by myself. It's other people's fault for barging in front of me!"

When it comes to change, we all have excuses that are so deeply embedded in our way of thinking that it's hard to see them for what they are:

- "I work hard all day, and I'm so stressed—food is my only pleasure!"
- "If I don't starve myself, I'll gain weight. The control I have over food feels powerful since I have no control in other areas of my life."
- "I need to gorge on food so I can be filled up. Food fills the emptiness inside me."

- "I have a fat gene! I was predestined to look this way."

The excuses are endless. I've lived many years of my life reciting them. But if Jesus were to face you today and ask, "Do you want to get well?" what would you immediately say to Him? "Yes, but . . ."

In his book *Healing is a Choice*, Stephen Arterburn writes, "Can you imagine the despair of a life unlived, spent lying by a pool that never brought healing? Thirty-eight wasted years seeking something that never happened as he tried the same thing over and over again with absolutely no results."[1] Like a compulsive overeater's dieting, an anorexic's refusal to give up discipline abuse, and a bulimic's perpetual purging, the habits handicap us to a point of compliant paralysis.

Arterburn goes on to say, "Asking a man who has been ill for thirty-eight years if he wants to be healed is not a bizarre question. I have worked with many people through the years who could have experienced healing but refused it. If Jesus had asked if they wanted to be healed, they might have answered no."

The truth is that we get something from the habits we choose to hang on to. Some people remain overweight so they can stay hidden. They use their weight as a protective wall that keeps people out. Being overweight invites a war within, where taste buds are the victors. Regardless of health or sane choices, if a large meal, drinks, and dessert are what's craved, that is what's ingested—period! Guilt may follow, but nothing wins out over the taste buds' immediate demands.

In an anorexic's mind, the need to control food intake and exercise always overrides reason. The reward may be bulging bones and clothes that fall off.

For a bulimic, the reward may be the golden short-cut of eating whatever is wanted compulsively, only to throw it up later so it won't stick. None of these disordered mind patterns are based on truth, yet they dominate behavior. These choices make it hard to honestly answer, "Yes, I want to get well."

You know in your heart when you're ready to change. This doesn't mean that you won't have failures or times of temptation. These are part of the mosaic of healing. It's an attitude, a willingness to look at yourself and let this destructive part of your life be cleaned out once and for all. I'm not talking about another diet, food program, doctor's recommendation, or *Seven Easy Steps to Control*. We've tried these things and either failed at them or, from an anorexic's perspective, abused the discipline. I'm talking about a decision to move toward freedom at all costs. Jesus asks *you* now, "Do you want to get well?" He never forces you or tricks you into anything. He gently but confidently says, "Come to Me all who are weary and heavy-laden, and I will give you rest. Take My yoke upon you and learn from Me, for I am gentle and humble in heart. . . . For My yoke is easy and My burden is light" (Matthew 11:28-30).

William Barclay adds, "The man had waited for thirty-eight years and it might well have been that hope had died and left behind a passive and dull despair. When we have intensity of desire and determination to make the effort, hopeless though it may seem, the power of Christ gets its opportunity, and with Him we can conquer what for long has conquered us."[2]

LOOKING WITHIN

God understands the pain you live with, the mental anguish you feel when you realize you want to be well but don't know where to begin or how to let go of the behaviors that are destroying you. Ask yourself these questions:

1. Is food a dominating, overwhelming force in my life?
2. Do my eating patterns affect my moods or the way I feel about myself?

3. Does the way I eat or think about food alienate me or make me feel shameful before God?

4. Do I view others in an obsessive or jealous way because of their weight or body shape?

I remember a time when I would have undeniably answered each of these questions yes! Food controlled my life and dominated my moods. I was filled with self-hatred and was jealous of women I felt had no trouble with eating or body image. I cried out to God 27 years ago when I was on the verge of suicide. I battled cycles of anorexia and compulsive overeating so severe that I seriously wanted to give up trying and take my own life. I saw no hope. There was no end in sight, and I felt an ever-present loneliness because I was too embarrassed and ashamed to share my heartache with anyone else. The pain and hatred I felt toward myself intensified until I couldn't take it any longer.

Looking back, I see that I began dieting during my sophomore year of college. I was a bit overweight at the time and hated the way I looked. I had seen in myself patterns of compulsive overeating in high school but nothing that seemed to control me. I would periodically binge but then soon forget about food and move on to something else. I can't say that I honestly know where I crossed the line into compulsion, but I do remember at one point thinking, *This is sick. Something is really wrong with me!*

One night I went to a sorority party with some girlfriends. On our way, we stopped at the store to get snacks. My friends and I gathered around the food, trying a little bit of everything: candy, chips, Pop Tarts—a real smorgasbord of healthful delights! As the night went on, I found I could not move away from the food. I was drawn by a force I couldn't seem to stop. I didn't want to eat it—I was stuffed—but I kept shoveling it in. Later that night I was over the toilet throwing up—not because

I forced myself to get sick but because my body couldn't handle all the food I had slammed down in a food-drunk rage.

I continued with constant binges and weight gain that entire semester of school. When I went home for Christmas vacation, I vowed to diet my eating into submission. I followed a well laid-out diet book perfectly and began my months—which turned into years—of starvation. What started out as something healthful and beneficial turned into the most destructive force in my life. I had been on dozens of diets before, including a strict banana diet in which I had headaches so severe that even the monkeys at the zoo would have held their heads and cringed! Typically, I started out with enthusiasm, but after a couple of days I was right back to my old habits.

This time was different. I began to see success and weight loss, and my self-confidence soared. Months passed, and in my severe dieting I rarely allowed myself more than 800 calories a day. During that time I noticed that some of my friends became concerned. I viewed their worry as jealousy and paid no attention to their warnings. Frankly, I loved my new sense of power and self-control. What I thought was discipline to be applauded soon began to choke me as I shriveled into a boney shape. I worked that summer at a health club, exercising all day long. Everything was perfect in my eyes as I was nearing my goal—the weight I been when I was about 11 years old. I had one normal menstrual period over the course of two years, and during that period I fainted. I quickly sprang up from being sprawled on the floor and simply chalked it up to overexertion and cramps.

My real mental anguish began when I returned to school the following fall. It was my junior year of college, and I was starting at a new school, San Diego State University. Weight began to creep back on once I started going to classes rather than working out all day. My entire face broke out with uncontrollable acne, something I had never struggled with before. Doctors later told me that my body was shutting down due to malnutrition and stress. I had learned to put my confidence in my outward appearance, and that confidence was being stripped away, leaving me lurching into a slow spiral of hatred and bizarre behavior.

For months, every time I looked in a mirror I wanted to take my fingernails and scratch off my face. I visualized doing this and rehearsed my hatred whenever I caught a glimpse of myself. The clothes I purchased when rail thin no longer fit, and the daily routine of getting dressed was a mental nightmare. The lies I recited wounded my heart and paralyzed me like a deer struck by a hunter's arrow.

"You're so ugly. You'll never be pretty again!"

"You have no self-control. You're useless!"

"You're a fat pig. If people knew the real you, they'd shudder!"

I saw no way out of my misery, and on the verge of suicide one morning, I went into my roommate's room and sat on her bed. She had a picture of Jesus smiling handsomely on her wall. I looked at it and helplessly said, *Jesus, whoever you are, if you're real, make yourself known to me. You're the last hope I have.*

There was no one pushing vague religion on me. No rules, regulations, traditions, or ideologies—just a simple, childlike plea for help. I had grown up going to church and trying hard to follow all the rules. The image I had of a far-away Savior in stone statues, stoically standing with His face down, was blinding. Could this person rescue me from danger? Was He more than a religious symbol and worthy of my trust? I put Him to the test and said, "Show yourself to me. You're the last hope I have."

As I finished these heart sobs, I felt as though the guilt and condemnation that had bound me for a lifetime finally had a foe. I hoped that the distorted mental image I had of myself, food, and appearance would be reckoned with, torn down, and rebuilt. But on a deeper level I knew I had to tell myself the truth. My life was full of self-deception, and I needed to admit it.

One of the toughest battles we face with disordered eating is the realization that we're deceived. Self-deception is debilitating, because it keeps us from seeing ourselves as we really are. When we're wrapped in the blanket of self-deception, as cozy as it sometimes seems to be, the truth of God is choked out. We entertain lies and rationalizations so readily that we become numb to the freedom of God's whisper.

Brennan Manning illustrates this deception powerfully as he tells a story in his book *The Importance of Being Foolish*. The man in the story struggles with alcoholism. The choices he makes to protect his self-deception are staggering, and Manning paints the deception in this man's life with brilliant clarity.

Twenty-five men, all chemically dependent on alcohol or drugs, have gathered. Croesus O'Connor, a recovering alcoholic, is the head honcho—a trained counselor, skilled therapist, and senior member of the staff. He summons Max, a small, diminutive man, to sit alone in the center of the U-shaped group. Max is a nominal Christian, married with five children, owner and president of his own company, wealthy and affable, gifted with a remarkable poise. O'Connor begins the interrogation:

"How long you been drinking like a pig, Max?"

Max winces. "That's not quite fair."

"We'll see. Let's get into your drinking history. How much per day?"

"Well, I have two Marys with the men before lunch and two Martins when the office closes at 5:00. Then . . ."

"What in God's name are Marys and Martins?"

"Bloody Marys—vodka, tomato juice, a dash of Worcestershire—and Martinis—extra dry, straight up, ice cold, with an olive and lemon twist."

"Thank you, Mary Martin. Go on."

"The wife likes a drink before dinner. Got her hooked on Martinis years back." Max smiles. "You understand that. Right, guys?" No one responds. "We have two drinks then, and two drinks before bed."

"Eight drinks a day, Max?" Croesus inquires.

"That's right. Not a drop more, not a drop less."

"You're a liar!"

Max is not ruffled. "I'll pretend I didn't hear that. Been in business twenty-eight years. People know my word is my bond. Built my reputation on veracity, not mendacity."

At this point in the story Max is asked if he ever keeps booze in the house. He laughs at the question as he explains that he has a fully stocked bar, used for entertaining, and cases of extra booze in the garage. When pressed further, he finally admits that he also keeps a bottle in his nightstand, one in his suitcase, another in his bathroom cabinet, and three more bottles at the office for entertaining.

O'Connor senses that Max is still hiding and picks up the phone to make a call. He calls a man from Max's hometown who tends a bar that Max frequents. After assuring the bartender that his information is sacred and being shared with the permission of his family, O'Connor asks him to tell roughly how much Max drinks each day. The bartender shares that Max drops a hundred bucks in there every day—drinking eight martinis and a variety of other drinks. At this point Max loses it as he jumps up and starts screaming profanities.

But the best is still to come. One of the group members asks Max if he has ever been unkind to one of his kids. Max settles back into a masked veneer and explains how close he is to his kids. As a matter of fact, he has just taken his boys on a fishing trip. O'Connor tells Max he isn't talking about that. He presses him to find the answer to the unkindness question. Max becomes silent for a moment and then quietly shares that he does have an unkind memory that he senses, but he can't exactly remember what happened. He just knows that it involves his nine-year-old daughter last Christmas Eve. O'Connor picks up the phone again and dials his hometown, this time speaking with his wife.

"Croesus O'Connor calling, ma'am. Your husband just told me he was unkind to your daughter last Christmas Eve. Can you give us the details?"

A soft voice fills the room. "Yes, I can tell you. Our daughter, Debbie, wanted a certain pair of shoes for Christmas. On the afternoon of the twenty-fourth, my husband drove her downtown, gave her forty dollars, and told her to buy whatever she wanted. That's what she did. When she got back in the truck, she kissed Max and told him he was the best daddy in the world. He was probably preening himself like a peacock and decided to celebrate on the way home. He stopped at a tavern near here and told Debbie he'd be right out. It was a clear, cold day, about eighteen degrees, so Max left the motor running and locked both doors so no one could get in. It was a little after three in the afternoon and . . ." Silence.

The sound of heavy breathing. Her voice grows faint. She is fighting back tears. "My husband came out of the bar at midnight. He was drunk. The motor had stopped, and the windows were frozen shut. Debbie was badly frostbitten on both ears and her fingers. When we got her to the hospital, the doctors had to operate. They amputated the thumb and forefinger in her right hand. She'll be deaf the rest of her life."[3]

Max begins to sob hysterically at this revelation of his true self. But no sympathy is given. He is finally looking at himself with all his excuses, insanity, and lies.

This stunning encounter with self-deception takes my breath away. Even now I can see how committed I am to my own deception. *At least my struggles with food weren't as bad as what this man did. I'm in good shape compared to him.* I smugly chant, feeling a little too proud. The truth is—self-deception always hurts someone. It may be a family member, a spouse, a friend, or simply me who pays a price. And make no mistake—there's always a price.

The sequel to Max's story is that he underwent a striking personality transformation. He was vulnerable, honest, and more affectionate. The night before he left the treatment center, another group member walked by his room. Max had tears streaming down his face as he quietly said, "I just prayed for the first time."

This was a gut prayer for Max. It was capable of transforming his heart and blinded eyes, just as my prayer was when I saw no hope for my trashed-out life. Healing is a process. It takes time and perseverance, but every small step or hushed cry is meaningful to God. "Do you want to get well?" Jesus asks. It's not a one-time question either. He keeps asking as long as He knows there's garbage in our lives that needs to be disposed of.

Oswald Chambers writes in his masterpiece *My Utmost for His Highest*, "God does not give us overcoming life. He gives us life to overcome."[4]

A LIVING HOPE FOR FREEDOM

Many people confide in me, saying that they've never equated freedom with disordered eating. The two just didn't seem to belong together. How does something as natural and necessary as eating become a recipe for addiction in our lives? Why do we beg for help yet struggle to let go of our habits?

Many years ago I pondered these questions before God. As a young woman I heard the term *saved* and, frankly, was irritated by the verbal slinging this term endured within the Christian community. In the eleventh edition of *Merriam-Webster's Collegiate Dictionary*, three of the definitions of *save* are

- Rescue from danger
- Preserve or guard from destruction or loss
- Redeem from sin[5]

My pondering led me to the realization that Jesus wants to rescue us from the danger of disordered eating. He can preserve us and guard us from the destruction of our bodies and minds and the loss of capacity to hear the truth about ourselves. And finally, He redeems us from sin.

We tend to have a grave misunderstanding of the word *sin*. The word itself signifies a weakened state of human nature in which the self is estranged from God. I was taught as a child that a sin was each singular act I committed that was wrong. Some sins were worse than others, and some were so bad that I could never recover from them. What a revelation it was to discover the biblical meaning of sin! It's a massive Grand Canyon separating a holy God from a stained human heart. The life and death of Jesus built a safe bridge over the canyon—a bridge that leads to wholeness and health.

In the book *Having a Mary Heart in a Martha World*, Joanna Weaver explains sin with clarity: "The very definition of sin is separation from God. So no matter what I do, if I use it as an excuse to hold God at arm's length, it is sin. I need to confess and repent of it so I can draw close to the Lord once more."[6]

The destruction of compulsive overeating, anorexia, bulimia, laxatives, diet pills, and yo-yo dieting is too much to bear on your own. That's why hospitals and clinics that treat people on a mere physical basis have an insignificant recovery rate. Many people I know have shared with me that they left some of these programs in a worse state than when they entered. But we have a living hope for freedom, not merely behavior modification or another food and exercise plan.

> Behold, the eye of the LORD is on those who fear Him, On those who hope for His lovingkindness, to deliver their souls from death And to keep them alive in famine. Our soul waits for the LORD; He is our help and our shield. For our heart rejoices in Him, Because we trust in His holy name. Let Your lovingkindness, O LORD, be upon us, according as we have hoped in You *(Psalm 33:18-22)*.

NO LOOKING BACK

The invalid in the gospel of John needed to trust in the man who was speaking freedom over his life. When he heard Jesus say, "Get up!" he had to believe this man wasn't nuts or teasing him for sport. To tell a man who's been hurt for 38 years to get up is bold. It's crazy and adventurous—a perfect description of how God can work in our lives if we let Him.

The next thing he heard was "Take up your mat." This demanded movement on his part. He couldn't choose to lie there *and* get well at the same time. He had to physically move toward freedom and use the limbs that had been rendered powerless for so long.

And finally, he had to let go of his past. Jesus said, "Take up your mat and walk." Essentially He told him, "Pick up what you've been lying on—bad habits, poor choices, destructive lies, self-deception—and start fresh." It was his chance to walk with a restored body and mind into a new life, to kick up formerly twisted limbs and dance. But here's the punch. He had to be willing to trust that Jesus was real and able to transform him. He then had to actively move his body toward freedom and let go of the mat he was accustomed to lying on.

Are you ready to take up your mat and walk? There's no greater joy or journey than a life lived in utter belief that God is bigger than our infirmity.

Trust Him, move with Him, and let go.

Personal Morsels

I've often thought that when people preach to me I internalize a portion of what they say, but when they share their stories with me, I'm drawn to their very souls. Our stories are uniquely ours, filled with pain and triumph. Sue Monk Kidd, best-selling author of *The Secret Life of Bees*, writes, "Creating story is an act of self-knowing. Through the lens of story we see the mystery of ourselves more clearly. Knowing who I am hinges on remembering who I have been in the past and embracing the hope of who I may be in the future. Story allows us to enter the tension between memory and hope."[7]

What's your story? When did you begin to feel out of control with food? What is your hope for the future?

I would like to challenge you to put your story on paper. As the events are transferred into this book, pray for the honesty and the wisdom of the Holy Spirit. My prayer for you is that as you write, your wounds and scars will be exposed so that as you learn and understand the truth, it will replace the blemish of disordered eating.

Write your story here:

_____

_____

_____

_____

_____

_____

_____

_____

_____

_____

_____

_____

_____

_____

_____

_____

_____

_____

_____

_____

Place a sticky note on the following scriptures in your Bible, or highlight them as a reference for strength and clarity.

John 5:6

How is Jesus proposing this to me today?

_____

_____

_____

_____

_____

_____

_____

_____

How have I ignored this invitation?

_____

_____

_____

_____

_____

_____

Psalm 107:19-20

What destructions can God deliver me from?

_____

_____

_____

_____

_____

How can He save me from my distresses when I cry out to Him?

_____

_____

_____

_____

_____

_____

TWO

An Honest Look at What's Eating You

One of the first areas in which we need to recognize truth, with God's help, is how we view our relationship with food. After suffering for years with disordered eating, I felt I was a victim being swallowed by an incurable force. Most books I read called my struggle a disease. Every time I thought about my battle with food as a disease, a sense of hopelessness overwhelmed me.

One day as I stood in my kitchen holding bags of fat-free chips and a box of Honey Nut Cheerios, I realized that I had made food my craven enemy. I suddenly had the urge to scream, "The God I love says I can have life and life abundantly! This isn't life! It's a hellish prison—and I have to break out!" I quickly packed up my small children and drove to a bookstore close to my home. Sitting on a bottom shelf with a plain, un-attractive cover, a title jumped out at me that demanded my attention—*The Diet Alternative*, by Diane Hampton.[1]

I took the small book home and read it from cover to cover. The title of the first chapter was "Deliverance from Gluttony." *Yuck!* I thought. *The word* gluttony *is a bit harsh*. I looked up the word and was stunned to see its meaning. "Glutton: one given habitually to greedy and voracious eating and drinking."[2]

As harsh as the word sounds, it's true. Gluttony is at the heart of most disordered eating, and surprisingly the Bible ad-dresses it directly. Proverbs 23:20-21 says, "Do not be with the heavy drinkers of wine, or with gluttonous eaters of meat; for the heavy drinker and the glutton will come to poverty."

Growing up with alcoholic parents, I had firsthand knowl-edge of what heavy drinkers look like, but to see that both the glutton and drunkard will come to poverty shocked me. Most people readily agree that drunks need help cleaning up their lives, but gluttons can live under the radar. Obese people are looked at as jolly, happy on the inside, and even commended for not being concerned with outside appearances. An anorexic may be complimented for discipline and lack of interest regarding food, when truthfully an anorexic is gluttonous in his or her mind, because food consumes every thought, even though it's not consumed.

Bulimics will gluttonously overeat and then feel the need to purge their bodies of the food so it won't stick. And the woman who curses the five to thirty pounds she wants to lose gluttonously plots and plans repeated diet oaths, only to end up angry when control seems futile.

Most of this behavior is played out secretly, so outward appearances remain unscathed. Unlike the drunk, gluttons may waste years telling themselves their behavior isn't that bad.

In *The Diet Alternative*, Diane Hampton shares that after reading countless diet books, undergoing self-hypnosis, and visiting a psychologist and a weight doctor, she recognized that there was still something driving her to act compulsively toward food. The driving force inside her was *sin*. Hampton relates Paul's letter to the Roman church to the intense struggle to gain power over food's control.

> I don't understand myself at all, for I really want to do [eat] what is right, but I can't. I do [eat] what I don't want to—what I hate. I know perfectly well that what I am doing [eating] is wrong, and my bad conscience proves that I agree with these laws I am breaking [condemnation is a constant companion of a compulsive eater]. But I can't help myself, because I'm no longer doing it. It is sin inside me that is stronger than I am that makes me do these evil things [binge, purge, starve]. No matter which way I turn I can't make myself do right [eat right . . . diet programs, psychology]. I want to, but I can't. Now if I am doing what I don't want to, it is plain where the trouble is: sin still has me in its evil grasp (*Romans 7:15-20*, TLB).[3]

Now before you throw this book against the wall in confusion, stay with me as I explain this concept. A precious woman struggling with severe anorexia and bulimia once cried to me, "So now, on top of all my failure, you're calling me a sinner?" Well—yes. This was in sharp contrast to the treatment programs and therapy sessions she attended where she was labeled a victim of a lifelong disease and given the mere hope of walking a tightrope of control regarding food for the rest of her life. When gluttony is recognized in our lives, there's only one remedy, as Paul attests to in Romans: *a Savior.*

When I read that gluttony was a sin problem, for the first time in my life I felt I had hope. I knew that Jesus claimed, "You shall know the truth, and the truth shall set you free" (John 8:32, NKJV), but I spent most of my time shackled to the darkness of lies and compulsion that sin held me bound to. I also knew that Jesus died for my sins. He crushed them on the Cross. So if the truth could set me free, and the Cross could crush my sin, there had to be hope for a new way of living—not a circus of behavior modification but true and lasting freedom from gluttony's hold. Oswald Chambers writes, "Sin is a fundamental relationship; it is not wrong doing, it is wrong being: deliberate and emphatic independence of God."[4]

My "wrong being" with food trickled into every area of life's domain: my self-image, my view of sexuality, my social etiquette, and my view of hope. How can we give lip service to a great God yet live independent of His power, grace, and freedom? This question stung my heart as I pondered the possibility of being truly fed and free.

THE PRINCIPLE OF SOWING SEEDS

The Bible is filled with guidelines that we can follow to help live the way God intended us to. I call these guidelines *principles*. One of the best principles I've studied regarding food is one that Hampton exposed as she connected food to the principle of sowing seeds to God. The power of the Word of God to change my heart, habits, and attitude once again became evident as I studied this scripture:

> Do not be deceived, God is not mocked; for whatever a man sows, this he will also reap. For the one who sows to his own flesh shall from the flesh reap corruption, but the one who sows to the Spirit shall from the Spirit reap eternal life (*Galatians 6:7-8*).

Sowing and *reaping*—how can these ancient-sounding agricultural words help in the healing of disordered eating? *Sowing* is a word used many times throughout the Bible to describe the action of scattering seeds, then nurturing and caring for their growth. Jesus himself used this term often when He explained principles to the disciples. Here, in his letter to the Galatians, Paul highlights that whatever persons sow—what they take their time doing, put their efforts into—will be what their lives reflect. He goes on to say that if we sow to the flesh—our own desires, appetites, and dangerous habits devoid of God's hand—we'll reap destruction.

We make choices daily in our lives: what we'll eat, how we'll eat, how much or how little we'll eat, which are literally the seeds we're sowing toward food. To a normal person who is not obsessed with food, these choices are natural, simple, and unrestricted. To someone struggling with disordered eating, these seeds are sown to the destruction of life.

Eating—sowing—to the flesh involves eating consistently when you're not hungry, bingeing secretly, throwing up after eating, using laxatives or diet pills to control weight, dieting on and off for a lifetime, starving and living within a limited regime of food allotments, and not eating a normal meal with family or friends. Eating to the flesh leads to destruction, and we know how destruction feels—empty, hopeless.

Now let's look at the second part of this powerful scripture in Galatians. The result of sowing to the Spirit is life. But what does it mean to sow to the Spirit? In his letter to the believers in Rome, Paul writes, "So then, brethren, we are under obligation, not to the flesh, to live according to the flesh—for if you are living according to the flesh, you must die; but if by the Spirit you are putting to death the deeds of the body, you will live" (Romans 8:12-13).

Paul doesn't mean you must physically die if you're living according to the flesh. He's referring to making those ugly, destructive behaviors die, killing them and putting them to death so you can truly live by the Spirit. It's a process that starts with logical, sensible actions and the supernatural help of God himself. Sowing seeds to the Spirit literally kills disordered eating.

"For the mind set on the flesh is death, but the mind set on the Spirit is life and peace" (Romans 8:6). Put yourself and your choices regarding your habits with food within the context of sowing seeds. Look at the simple fact that you and I have two choices: we can sow seeds to God, which produces the sweet aroma of life and peace, or sow seeds to the flesh, which results in pain and destruction. Remember that God doesn't love us any more when we succeed or any less when we fail. His love for us is like a mighty fortress and can never be weakened by behavior. Because He loves us so fiercely, He desperately wants us to live free from these shackles and chains of destruction.

After I read Galatians 6:7-8, I began thinking about how I could sow seeds to God within my daily eating. I was struck by the notion that every seed I choose to sow to the Spirit is welcome and precious in God's sight. I once heard author and speaker Beth Moore mention that "God is not looking for spiritual giants. He's looking for believers who believe for a change."

SEED–SOWING

All of us have different habits and heartaches regarding our choices with food, so as you read this section, reflect on how you can sow seeds according to your own needs. If you struggle with overeating during particular times of the day, you might choose that time to sow as a seed to the Spirit. For instance, many people feel fine with their eating throughout the day, but at night they begin to feel out of control with food and will binge until they fall into bed, only to get up and repeat the pattern the next day. Some may find themselves up two or three times during the night, rummaging through the refrigerator and stuffing themselves, then returning to bed.

For me, preparing a meal was a danger zone. As I cooked, I shoveled food into my mouth. By the time the meal was on the table, I had already eaten the equivalent of two meals. So this was the time I chose to begin sowing my seed to God. As I prepared a meal for my family, I thanked God for His strength and power. I looked at that time as my "fast" to the Lord. It was difficult at first, because my hands were on autopilot, ready to cram food into my mouth. I slowly and profoundly repeated a phrase that many women say is one of their most helpful tools: "I don't do that anymore!"

Initially, my head played games with me as I tried to break this habit and give it to God as seed. *It's no big deal. You're hungry, and a little food while you're cooking won't hurt you.* I knew differently. I knew that my bingeing was hurting me and setting me up for other failures with food. As I vowed to offer this time as seed, I began to experience the pleasure of actually feeling hungry at a meal, and I noticed that after sowing that time to God, my sowing spilled over into other times and attitudes toward food. I was able to sow seeds during incessant snacking, overeating, secret binges in my car or back pantry, and the constant nag of a twisted view of my body.

Sowing seeds to the Spirit can be applied to any destructive behavior associated with disordered eating. If you suffer from bulimia, your anguish is probably most attached to the habit of throwing up. For some, the desire to purge doesn't necessarily follow only after a binge. The actual ritual of throwing up has become such a habit that several lunges over the toilet daily are not uncommon. If this is part of your disordered pattern, my prayer for you is that you realize that you can stop this behavior and have the normal life you've longed for.

Spirit Seeds
- Food secrets are exposed
- Understanding the truth about our bodies and habits
- Offering to God specific times we engage in damaging behavior, choosing to change our actions and habits
- Filling our minds with scripture and affirming phrases

Flesh Seeds
- Hiding and lying about food
- Denying that habits are destructive
- Continuing behaviors that lead to guilt, shame, and secrecy
- Reciting lies in the mind and remaining hopeless

To apply seed-sowing to purging, first realize that the journey toward healing produces maturity, and this doesn't happen overnight. Start by sowing small, life-changing seed to God. If you throw up a couple of times a day, choose to sow one of those times to the Lord. I know this isn't easy, but it's essential to make the choice to start somewhere. When the urge to vomit strikes, recite, "I don't do that anymore!" and replace that time over the toilet: read or write scripture, write in a journal, go for a walk, hold your child, play a good song, clean something—anything—to fill that space you would normally hang over the toilet. I realize this may sound trite, as if I don't understand the conflict that rages in your mind and body when a ravenous habit seeks to destroy you. I *do* understand. I've been in your shoes, worn and downtrodden. I understand the disgust and hopelessness—I've cried the same bitter tears. It feels like a battle, because it *is* a battle. But you can thank God that He is stronger than the urge you feel that leads to destruction.

By making the choice not to throw up at that specific time, you're sowing a seed to the Spirit for life rather than to the flesh for destruction. It may seem small and insignificant, but it's beautiful and treasured by God. Continue to sow that particular time to God, and add seed to the other difficult times you face. Soon the destructive habit will be shattered.

Purging doesn't encompass only throwing up. It can also be the panic you feel if you can't exercise during a particular day. A routine of intense walking, running, or cycling that's interrupted often feels like failure to a bulimic purger. I'm not talking about the joy that being active and athletic brings. I recently began training with some friends for a sprint triathlon. I'm no world-class athlete—I'm not even a serious local athlete. But I love the strength I feel when I'm working out my body.

Everyone who works out in any capacity should feel a surge of confidence from the decision to make healthy choices in his or her life. The danger comes with a perversion of healthy exercise. I'm talking about an addiction to exercise that permeates and drives you to points of compulsive behavior. If you find yourself exercising at bizarre hours of the day or night or for lengths of time uncommon to a normal athlete, this is where your seed-sowing comes in. You can offer this extreme behavior to the Lord as seed, asking Him to replace it with a normal desire for health and fitness. Maybe you can call a friend instead of putting on sweats and heading for the gym. Maybe you can spend that time reading a good book or having some peaceful time with God instead of compulsively pushing yourself out the door to run.

There will be times of temptation when you want to return to your destructive habits rather than sowing seeds for life and freedom. You can expect those times. Knowing that times of temptation and battleground engagements are normal helps ease the mental anguish. You don't have to feel as though you're failing at a diet, a program, or a guided plan. When you sow seeds to God, the result is always peace and wisdom. Even when you fail or feel overcome by old habits, you're still moving forward if you're honestly seeking the wisdom God wants to give you regarding food.

An Old Testament scripture we can strap onto our backs as we engage in habit busting is "The eyes of the LORD move to and fro throughout the earth that He may *strongly support* those whose heart is completely His" (2 Chronicles 16:9, emphasis added).

In her book *Having a Mary Heart in a Martha World*, Joanna Weaver states, "Consistency, after all, doesn't mean perfection; it simply means refusing to give up."[5]

SOWING SEEDS IN ANOREXIC BEHAVIOR

If you're suffering from anorexic behavior, you can sow seeds in a different way. Your pain and struggle stems from a fear of eating and gaining weight, not the actual habit of overeating. Many people who battle anorexia were at one time a bit overweight. Success in dieting may have brought compliments and accolades, but as time passes and the need to lose weight ends, the restrictive behavior adhered to by an anorexic seems too precious to give up. Others may have started with a normal body weight, but normal isn't perceived as thin enough. Unrealistic lies and fear begin to haunt the anorexic, and before long the fear of food has become a dragon to be slain.

I've found that the best way to handle this fear is to make a list of the reasons you're afraid to eat. With your list of fears, include what living under a strict food allotment does for you. My list looked something like this:

- If I ingest any sugar or fat, I'll instantly gain weight.
- Without perfect discipline, my body will get fat.
- This is one area of my life I know I can control and see results. I need that control.
- This isn't a problem—it's a quality. Everyone would love to be able to control his or her food consumption as I do.
- Gaining weight is my enemy. Even being a normal or healthy weight is unacceptable for me.
- If I don't feel hungry, I'm failing.

These were just a few of the lies and fears that ran my life. Anorexia runs from a web of distortion that has gripped the mind so successfully that its prey is left disillusioned in the wake of the power of the lies. Our enemy, the evil one, is the master of disaster. He whispers a string of potent lies. With freakish submission, the anorexic believes the lies as they change and mold perceptions. Since anorexia stems from a tainted view of food and the body, sowing seeds to the Spirit involves recognizing these lies and fears for what they are and replacing them with truth.

Anorexics are known for their rituals. As a matter of fact, these rituals with food, weight, and exercise consume the mind of the anorexic. Determine which ritual or distortion plagues you most. It may be a vigorous exercise routine that follows the ingestion of even the smallest amount of food or a ritual of weighing yourself throughout the day to monitor your body's weight. It may be a strict restriction of any food that isn't a protein, fruit, or vegetable, or a wave of guilt if you eat anything that isn't healthful. If you're young, it may be the constant struggle between you and your parents. They try to get you to eat, and you fight them or sneak around them because they don't understand your fear. Or it might be the ritual of standing in front of the mirror and critically examining your body to find areas of fat to obsess about.

Whatever it is that plagues you most, you can *choose* to sow seeds to the Spirit for life and truth in your thinking rather than participating in the twisted lies mangling your behavior. Take one specific thing you do, and give it to God as seed. For example, if you desperately want to be free from excessive exercise and guilt when you're finished eating, rather than strapping on your sneakers, stop and take a deep breath. Get your Bible and a notebook, and write down word for word the lie you're telling yourself.

Lie: *I have to exercise now or I'll gain weight.*

Writing down the lie takes it out of your mind and puts it onto paper. Lies have a way of spreading like fire through brittle pine needles. Once the flame is ignited, it engulfs everything around it. I've put this lie to the test many times in my life. As a mother, teacher, writer, speaker, and wife, I've gone through many periods when I had little time to work out. Although exercise has always been something I love and believe in, some seasons of my life dictated less physical activity. By sowing seeds to the Lord regarding my eating, and consuming food sensibly and without compulsion, I've maintained the same weight for more than 19 years.

This lie, and many others like it, run women ragged. Once the lie is written down, sow seed to God by repeating *truth* followed by an *action*. You may want to write a scripture under the lie, such as "He has satisfied the thirsty soul, and the hungry soul He has filled with what is good" (Psalm 107:9).

The action that follows is how you talk back to the lie. You take charge of your mind by saying, "This lie says I have to work out now in order not to gain weight, but I know that God fills me with truth and what is good." Maybe your reaction will be to cut down the amount of time you feel you have to exercise or to do an activity totally unrelated to working out, such as reading a book, cleaning up, calling a friend, or taking a bath. I've heard women say they were amazed at how much time they gained in a day once they gave up this lie and others like it.

Sowing seed to the lies and perverted food systems that govern anorexic thinking is powerful. If this is an area where you struggle, it may take some time to untwist what's taken months or years to settle into your thought patterns. But each seed you sow is honored by God. Ask the Holy Spirit to show you the lies you must release—and then scrub your mind clean of them.

SOWING SEEDS IN OUR NUMB ZONE BEHAVIOR

For all of us who have suffered from disordered eating of any kind, there's a place we disappear into that I call *the numb zone*. It's the mental state we retreat to when we hide and sneak what we consume, a place where we shut out the people we love in order to numbly carry out our strange behaviors with food.

One friend shared with me that drive-through restaurants were at the heart of her compulsion. She hit the drive-through on her way home from work or gorged on cheeseburgers, fries, and a milkshake late in the evening after eating a plain salad for dinner with her family. There's an initial buzz of a secret tryst that pushes us forward in these moments, and we numbly comply like a hypnotized child. Drive-through deception is common among those who struggle with disordered eating. There's a deceiving allure to pulling up to a speaker that doesn't know you, ordering food you don't feel good about eating, and consuming it in the private confines of your car. Yet after the thrill of sneaking food is gone—and it lasts only for a few minutes—you're left with a guilty conscience, a lonely heart, and an upset stomach.

One of my numb zones followed my trips to the grocery store, where I had shopped alone. As I drove home, I ripped open bags of chips and cereal and stuffed their contents into my mouth. I then hid the bags or boxes so no one would see that that I had eaten from them.

I've often said that during binges, throwing up, or compulsive exercise, one who suffers from disordered eating doesn't even answer the phone or the door. That's the numb zone, where the consumption or rejection of food reigns. When we're in the numb zone, it seems that God is also locked out. It's too embarrassing to let anyone see us in this surreal state, so we shut people and God out of these moments of our lives. Ironically, these are the very moments God wants to be a part of. He's there whether we invite Him in or not. He looks at us with love and compassion, not disgust or judgment, as we may imagine.

In an article in *Prevention* magazine Geneen Roth describes her plight with breaking out of the numb zone. "Many years ago I made a commitment to myself that I would not be sneaky about food or my feelings ever again. Now, if I am binge-ing, and my husband Matt walks into the room, I say, 'Oh, hi. I felt like eating a lot, so here I am. Want a bite?'"[6]

You're probably thinking right now that you could never do that. Here's where seed-sowing comes in. Whatever numb zone behavior you participate in—bingeing, sneaking food, ly-ing to others about food, secretly throwing up, weighing your-self compulsively, or pretending to eat when you're really starv-ing yourself—take this behavior and let God in. Invite Him, speak to Him, and even praise Him when you're in the numb zone. This is your seed to the Spirit.

Some people have told me they do talk to God in these times. One woman shared, "I scream, *Why can't you help me, God? Where are you?*" But this is barking at God, not talking to Him as we would an intimate loved one. When I began to sow seeds to God while I was in my numb zones, it went something like this: *God, I know I'm stuffing food into my face now and try-ing to hide from the family I love. I invite you into this moment. I know your truth can set me free. I love who you are and who you want me to be. Help me to walk toward freedom and truth in this next moment. Thanks for loving me even at my compulsive worst. I am yours.*

Sowing seeds in these moments feels like washing an in-fected wound. Instead of locking God and loved ones out, I sowed seed to invite them in. I told my husband, Bobby, about my behavior and the struggles I had with bingeing and starving. I was such a successful master of deceit that he was shocked initially. I confess that it was terrifying at first. I remember the night I was tempted to sneak ice cream, as had been my nightly habit. Instead, I sowed seed and rebelliously spoke to that lie, "I don't do that anymore!" I dished the ice cream out into a bowl—food-sneakers rarely use bowls or utensils—and sat down beside Bobby to eat it. After a few bites, I was satisfied. I remember my heart skipping as I realized, *This is what freedom feels like!*

You may wonder in what way sowing seeds to the Spirit differs from the discipline of dieting and food control. Seed-sowing is an act of *worship.* We often view worship as something reserved for the church pews on Sunday. The truth is—I do some of my worst worshiping on Sundays. I find myself examining the cute haircut of the woman in front of me or listening to the tender cries of a baby close by. Before you know it, I'm lost in my own thoughts and reflection. True worship is an act of humility and awe. It's when you say to God, *You are the greatest part of my life. You are my breath, my love, and my purpose. You are worthy of all praise and wonder forever.*

In his introduction to the Book of Revelation in *The Message,* Eugene Peterson masterfully describes worship. He explains how John, a pastor in the late first century, was deeply concerned with worship. Although he was banished to an island because of the threat of his Christian beliefs, John knew its value. He was worshiping God on a certain Sunday when the vision of Revelation came to him. Notice that he didn't need a choir, worship leaders, or church pews. It was an active choice—a state of mind that put John in a position to hear from God and love Him more deeply. Peterson says, "Worship shapes the human community in response to the living God. . . . Our times are not propitious for worship. The times never are. The world is hostile to worship. The Devil hates worship. As The Revelation makes clear, worship must be carried out under conditions decidedly uncongenial to it. Some Christians even get killed because they worship.[7]

Although we may not die worshiping, sowing seeds in a worshipful state can bring death to an area of our lives that's been under enemy siege. When we offer our attitude, time, habits, or cherished rituals to God, it's an act of worship unparalleled. All that's needed is a willing heart that longs to please God more than continuing in empty ruts of behavior.

In her bible study *Stepping Up: A Journey Through the Psalms of Ascent*, Beth Moore shares a poignant story about seed-sowing. She traveled to the war-torn country of Angola to do relief work with her husband, Keith. In the midst of starving men, women, and children who had little or no contact with the world outside their village, Beth was told that the people would often devour hard seeds as meals instead of planting them to garnish a harvest.[8]

In other words, they ate what was sent to save them instead of planting it to produce a lasting crop of immeasurable benefit.

Isn't this true in our lives too? We often gobble down the content of the Bible, a great sermon, a book, or a Bible study, only to have it produce nothing in our lives. We're eating the seed without sowing it for lasting impact.

Sowing is active. An active state is different than a passive state, because passivity resists making a move or change. Dieting is passive, because after a designated time frame or cycles of weight-loss-then-gain, this passive behavior shuts down and resents itself. Sowing seeds to the Spirit for life is different. It's a choice to move toward a God who proclaims freedom for the captive and light for the blind. Sowing seeds is an action we choose over another action—whether it's habitually overeating, distorted views of our body and our relationship with food, or numb zones in which we shut out God and family. It's an action that God honors and welcomes. It's a choice to let go of our past habits and compulsion and move into a new way of thinking about food.

SOWING SEED TO LOSE WEIGHT

My guess is that if you're reading this book, you're probably struggling with your weight. Perhaps you've been considerably overweight for years and you've grown accustomed to the way weight shadows your self-esteem and outlook. Or you may struggle with the constant cycle of dieting and overeating, trying to lose the same five to thirty pounds you hate. Failure, or the fear of it, is the number-one enemy in the mind of a yo-yo dieter or someone who has been overweight for a long time. "I hardly eat anything!" one overweight friend cried to me. "It's like my body is stuck at this weight no matter what I do!"

I once heard a preacher say, "Never let the sense of failure defeat your new actions." New action is what's needed. Each new seed you sow is potent and life-changing. One of the ways you can apply seed-sowing to the desire to lose weight is to be a food detective, noticing the times during the day when you indulge mindless eating. *Mindless eating* is that bag of chips that disappears while you're watching television, the many bites of food that never make it to the table when you prepare a meal or help small children eat. It's the extra donut or bagel at work after you already had a bowl of cereal for breakfast at home. It's the bread, full plate of pasta, plus dessert at the restaurant. It's secretly cruising through the drive-through and gorging on food when no one sees.

To be aware of mindless eating, you have to get honest with yourself. If you're still fooling yourself with the attitude of "I'm not so bad—I don't eat as much as [enter name of friend or relative here]," you won't win this battle. This is about *your* freedom. Do away with excuses.

During a meeting of educators I attended recently, the presenter challenged the audience with some new ideas. She boldly said, "You have to remove the 'Yeah, buts' from your vocabulary."

"Yeah, but I don't have the genes to be thin."

"Yeah, but my metabolism just isn't fair."

"Yeah, but I love food. It's my one joy in life."

"Yeah, buts" get in the way of seed-sowing and healing. They have to go.

If you long to lose weight, choose seeds that can be sown for that purpose. After honestly evaluating your eating patterns and habits, pick a time you'll use as seed. If you overeat regularly during the late afternoon, sow that time to God. Diane Hampton talks about sowing seed from breakfast to dinner. When she wanted to lose weight, she ate a normal breakfast, then sowed seed to God throughout the day until dinner. At dinner she sat down and enjoyed a good meal, not dry lettuce and Melba toast.

When I feel I need to drop a few pounds, I simply cut back on how much I eat and sow seeds when I might ordinarily snack. I used to ration every bite and vehemently count calories. Now, if I want a turkey sandwich for lunch, I have it. But during seed-sowing for weight loss, I'll make half a sandwich. I enjoy every bite, and because I'm not dieting, I know I can eat what I want in moderation.

You may be thinking, *If I could control my desire to overeat, I would. If I allow myself to eat what I want, I'll gain weight.* This may be true with your former *dieting mentality*, but remember that seed-sowing is a spiritual act of worship. It's different than dieting resolve, which wanes with the temptation of a hot fudge sundae. We've controlled, forced, denied, and lamented food for so long that to sow seeds for weight loss may seem ridiculous.

A precious woman came up to me recently and shared that she had lost 25 pounds. She had sowed her tricky times of the day to God by refusing to eat during meal preparation and not snacking after dinner in the evenings. About a year later, she wrote me to let me know that the weight loss had been permanent. She couldn't believe the freedom she felt to eat sensibly and honestly.

Sowing seed may look different from one person to the next, but the result is the death of gluttony, and that's a funeral we would all like to attend.

Personal Morsels

Let's read again the scripture that's the basis of this chapter: Galatians 6:7-9. It's the cornerstone of *Truly Fed* and the anchor for behavioral change. Please look up this scripture in your own Bible, and mark it for further reference.

Do not be deceived, God is not mocked; for whatever a man sows, this he will also reap. For the one who sows to his own flesh will from the flesh reap corruption, but the one who sows to the Spirit will from the Spirit reap eternal life. Let us not lose heart in doing good, for in due time we will reap if we do not grow weary.

In what ways do you see yourself sowing to the flesh with food? Write out your flesh-sowing behaviors here.

_____

_____

_____

_____

_____

_____

_____

_____

_____

Many of us misunderstand the word *sin*. Definitions such as punishment, guilt, and damnation come to mind as we replay individual indiscretions and expect the slap on the wrist that reminds us of how bad we are. This was not Jesus' approach to sin. He didn't go after particular acts or behaviors; He went straight to the state of the heart. Consider the woman caught in the act of adultery. The "religious" men brought her to Jesus, gloating in the fact that this sin demanded that she be stoned to death under Jewish law. Jesus made a monumental statement when He looked at the gloaters and invited any of them who hadn't messed up to throw the first stone. One by one they left the scene, leaving only Jesus and the woman at the Temple. Chances are that she thought, *Now I'll get my punishment. Here it comes.* Instead, Jesus told her He didn't condemn her but asked that she change the direction of her life and sin no more (John 8).

What a radical difference this is from the image of sin that most of us carry with us: sin equals punishment, and punishment equals despair. The Bible refutes this image and makes it clear that sin is a state of separation from God, not a tally list of infractions. Take a moment to breathe a silent prayer, asking God to reveal your understanding of sin and the fear that may accompany it.

_____

_____

_____

_____

_____

_____

_____

_____

_____

_____

The second part of the Galatians principle involves sowing to the Spirit for life. What kind of seed can you offer God in the way you think about food and consume it? Write out how you can sow seeds to the Spirit for life.

_____

_____

_____

_____

_____

_____

_____

_____

_____

The last portion of this scripture encourages you not to lose heart in doing good, because you'll reap in due time if you don't grow weary. Remember that this is not a diet plan or food program—this is a change you're making in your *life*.

Most of us who have struggled with disordered eating are programmed in timeframes: "I'll try this for a while [Weight-Watchers, Jenny Craig, the latest diet craze, a new diet pill] and see how it works for me." Many people have initial success, but their minds remain victim to the prey of defeat and habitual rebellion. When you sow behavior and attitudes to the Spirit, how can you let go of time frames and not lose heart?

_____

_____

_____

_____

_____

_____

_____

_____

_____

_____

_____

THREE

What Are You Really Hungry For?

Can you pinpoint the last time you felt a normal sensation of hunger and then sat down to satisfy it?

I experienced years of twisted feelings and emotions toward hunger. For many years I binged uncontrollably throughout the day and night. Hunger was never the criteria for deciding how much to eat; compulsion and obsession drove me. I couldn't eat just two cookies—I had to eat the entire bag of cookies. If I didn't finish off the whole bag in one sitting, the thought of those cookies waiting to be eaten haunted me all day. I mindlessly reached for them until the bag was empty. I hated myself for doing it, but I felt I had no control over my actions. Later, when I began to diet and saw that I could stick to my disciplined plan, *control* became an obsession, and I substituted one harmful behavior for another.

If I wasn't experiencing severe hunger pains every night as I crawled into bed, I was angry with myself and silently promised I would do better the next day. From the moment my eyes opened the next morning, I planned my 800 calories for that day. I became incredibly angry if the day's activities led me off the track of sticking to my plan to consume that scant allotment of food.

For my birthday one year my sister prepared a special surprise dinner for me. I yelled at her because I had planned to eat a can of green beans and a cup of plain popcorn that night! Eating out inevitably turned into prolonged scrutiny of the menu so I could determine the plainest, most low-calorie combination of foods possible. Even intimate social settings where friends and family turned a watchful eye at my food choices didn't stop me. I was on a quest to starve myself, and nothing got in my way. Now that I'm free from the bondage of food, gluttony, and control, I'm amazed at how bizarre some of my actions were.

The truth is that hunger has a specific purpose in our lives. It's no accident that our bodies get hungry. God created us this way on purpose. He designed our bodies with a complex, miraculous digestive system. He equipped us with teeth, saliva, and taste buds to effectively ingest food and enjoy it. He also provided us with systems that use what we eat for fuel, store some of it for protection, and expel what our bodies don't need. Feeling hungry is natural. It's the way God planned for us to function.

I've often heard experts say that we deal with two types of hunger. The first type is a *body* hunger. This refers to the natural function of our bodies to feel hunger and then be fed.

We also have a *spirit* hunger. Everyone is made of flesh and spirit. Your spirit comes alive when you welcome Jesus into your heart. Because your spirit is alive, as well as your body, it, too, needs to be fed and nourished. Your body requires a variety of foods in sufficient quantities to satisfy its hunger. Your spirit needs communication with God (prayer), time spent reading and thinking about the Word of God, and relationship with others for it to grow and mature as designed. When these hungers aren't satisfied properly, disorder arises.

I believe there's a third category in addition to body and spirit hunger. This category is *emotional* hunger. Sometimes we eat to satisfy an emotional need. If we're angry or nervous, we eat to ease the tension. If we're lonely, food becomes a substitute companion. If we're bored or frustrated, we eat to fill time. Everyone, at one time or another, eats to satisfy an emotional need, but it is important to separate emotions from consistent, damaging eating patterns. Reaching for food may have begun as comfort or distraction from something painful. It made us feel better for a while, as an aspirin helps a headache. This pattern of thinking shifts and becomes dangerous when we continue to choose food rather than experience an unwanted emotion. We stuff or starve ourselves, making food the focus rather than living and experiencing the emotional challenges of life.

When feeling lonely or sad, we sometimes must sit with it and *feel* it rather than reaching for chips, sweets, or mocha lattes. Feeling our emotions can be difficult, because we're so accustomed to denying them and running from thing to thing or food to food in an attempt to forget how we feel.

Behavior becomes habit, and as we continue in the habit, its control grows and spills over into other areas of our lives. We are eating no longer in response to hunger but to feed a habit and to cover up a part of ourselves.

These habits may begin as overeating, but they can soon escalate into binges. For some, this opens the doors to forced vomiting or laxatives to try and get rid of what's been eaten. The next day begins with good intentions but ends up with acting out the habitual behavior. It all points back to the fact that we've lost what it means to experience true hunger.

One of the most helpful books I read regarding this is *Breaking Free from Compulsive Eating*, by Geneen Roth. I wonder if you relate to what she says about hunger:

> By the time I was twenty-eight I knew how many calories were in any food that was presented to me. I knew how to lose weight and how to gain weight. I knew how to maintain my weight. I knew how to diet and binge. But I didn't know when I was hungry. More painful, I didn't know it was okay to be hungry. Those of us who have spent months or years or decades dieting learn that someone else always knows better and that if we listen to what they tell us to eat, we will have the body they tell us we'll have. Unappetizing, unattractive, and at times nauseating combinations of food become palatable if they promise

slender arms and legs. When inevitably we break from the confinement of a diet, we are no closer to eating from hunger than we were when we were dieting. The first step in breaking free from compulsive eating is to eat when you are hungry.[1]

Eating when hungry sounds simple, so why is it so hard to do? It's hard because we've been programmed for years to listen to what everyone else says is right for our bodies. Diets dictate calories and carbohydrates and tell us what combinations of food to eat and when to eat them. We've heard the slogans all our lives: "Follow our book!" "Drink your meals!" "Use our products, and you, too, can have a perfect body!"

Even well-established groups that offer time for sharing and helping one another end in restrictive programs. Many people have shared with me the hopelessness they felt when they failed at these programs. Although some programs have a lot to offer, another food plan or dictated diet reaffirms our fears that we aren't capable of eating properly on our own.

If you feel panicked at the thought of losing a set of rules and regulations regarding eating, you're not alone. Believe me—I studied diets and diet books intensely for years, all under the guise of healthful living. In the end, those diets and diet books were still nothing more than obsession with food.

It may seem easier and more comfortable to follow a diet than it would be to learn about true hunger. In many ways it *is* easier, but when the allotted time for the diet is over, you're still left with the empty reality that you haven't dealt with food and hunger. When one chooses not to deal with this reality, it often leads to failure, insecurity, and fear of food.

God's desire is for you to live a happy, well-balanced, fulfilling life. His love, power, and comfort are endless. He created our bodies to experience hunger and to feel the joy of satisfying our hunger with an array of foods. Juicy fruits, hardy vegetables and proteins, even sweets were designed to satisfy our hunger and hankerings. Instead, many people substitute compulsive overeating for natural hunger. Anorexics deny hunger and even rage against it; bulimics gorge on food, knowing that they'll get rid of it later.

God describes these patterns of disordered eating as "yokes" around our jaws. In the Bible, the word *yoke* was used to describe oppression (Deuteronomy 28:48), hard service (1 Kings 12:4-14), bondage to sin (Lamentations 1:14), and legalistic ordinances (Galatians 5:1).

Hosea 11:4 offers us a life-changing invitation regarding the yoke of our attitudes and behavior toward food. God says, "I led them with the cords of a man, with bonds of love. And I became to them as one who lifts the yoke from their jaws; *and I bent down and fed them*" (emphasis added).

Can you imagine eating a meal with the Lord? Would you stuff food into your mouth and later excuse yourself to throw it up? Would you refuse food while He sat eating alone? Would you look at what He offered and reject it because it wasn't on your food plan?

Hosea says that *He* bends down and feeds us. *He* lifts the yoke from our jaws so we can eat freely and in true response to hunger. This scripture is both thrilling and surprising. I always felt that I must get this area of my life under control on my own. I sensed that God frowned upon my overeating and my abuse of control that resulted in anorexia. My warped image of God's not being involved in this area of my life made me feel as if I just needed to try harder, which I was already pushing myself to do. I really didn't integrate God's repeated messages of freedom in Scripture to my "yoke-driven" eating patterns.

What a comfort it was to see that God himself lifts the yoke from our jaws and feeds us! Although He didn't show up with a fork and a chair across the table from me, I began to sense His healing and presence in all food-related areas of my life. God can't be compartmentalized. He isn't with us only during the church-like times in our lives. He wants to be part of our eating, sleeping, dreaming, working, struggling, playing— all of it. He'll teach us about true hunger if we allow Him to. He longs to set us free.

LISTENING TO HUNGER

In order to develop your self-trust with food, you must first learn to listen to your body. I say *learn*, because it is a new experience to trust yourself to eat in response to hunger rather than compulsion. My prayer for you is that you will honestly begin to look at your eating patterns and not be completely overwhelmed by them.

One of the first steps in recognizing hunger is detecting the time frame in which you eat, how much you eat, and why you eat. Without knowing these three things, your mind stays fearful of the patterns that dictate your behavior. In the book *Inner Eating*, Shirley Billigmeier suggests a circle diagram to represent each act of eating.[2]

Every time you eat, even if it's a bite of something, you make a circle. The bigger the circle, the more food you ate. Here's an example of a day's diagram:

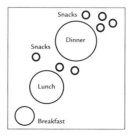

By diagramming and acknowledging the amounts of food you eat, the patterns that are problem areas for you can be seen in black and white rather than imagined. For some, the diagrams may show chaotic patterns.

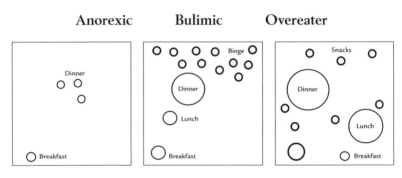

Anorexic   **Bulimic**   **Overeater**

There's space in the Personal Morsels section of this chapter for this activity. I recommend diagramming your food intake for several days. This gives you a clear picture of the choices you make with food.

Although the circle diagram may seem pointless to you, I recently tried it myself and was amazed by the number of times I eat during a day without acknowledging it as eating: finishing off part of a peanut butter sandwich left over on a child's plate, a few goldfish crackers here and there as I walked past the bag. I welcome anything that can help me gain knowledge and wisdom about the way I eat and the choices I make regarding food. It was refreshing to recognize my patterns without a trace of condemnation or guilt. Remember that Jesus said, "You shall know the truth, and the truth shall set you free" (John 8:32, NKJV). Don't be afraid of the truth. We must know the truth about our eating habits in order to be free of them.

As you draw your diagrams for a few consecutive days, you may want to jot down on the page why you choose food at that moment. Are you feeling angry? Bored? Lonely? It's during these times that we abandon hunger and eat to satisfy a different kind of need.

I've noticed that I often mark a transition in my day with food. During my teaching career, when my class moved from language arts instruction to math, we would have a snack. I usually felt quite hungry by that point in the morning, so it was fitting to eat a snack before lunch. But if I wasn't hungry, I would allow myself a bite of something or a drink I enjoy, marking the transition without turning to compulsive behavior.

I also notice that I tend to reach for food when I'm bored or lonely. This is when many of us long for purpose or community but grab a quick fix such as cookies, chips, cereal, or bread instead. Like aspirin to a multi-trauma patient, these trips to the fridge or cabinet don't really fix the pain of loneliness or boredom—they just divert it for a moment.

A good friend of mine shared how she felt around the holidays when she was showered with cards highlighting children and happy couples. She was single and led a life different than most of those around her. The loneliness and longing sometimes seemed overwhelming. She told me that when she felt such loneliness, she purposefully sat down and shared that time with God. She didn't allow herself to eat, run errands, jump on the treadmill, or watch Oprah. After she shared that time with Him, she got up and went ahead with her day. The loneliness maybe was and maybe wasn't still there, but the compulsion to numb it with food or activity was gone.

I came to realize that I'm terrified of being lonely or bored. I would rather fill myself with food or busyness than experience these emotions. But even Jesus himself was lonely at times. He traveled and worked intimately with a small band of men and women, but He often slipped away to mountaintops or quiet retreats to share with His Father the loneliness of being human.

We were created for purpose and community, but stuffing or starving ourselves to quench these longings is a diversion from true hunger.

RECOGNIZING YOUR HUNGRY/FULL SENSATION

If you haven't known true hunger for years, you might be wondering how you'll detect it and what you'll do with it once you know it's there. Many women and men have shared with me that they're afraid to be hungry. They fear that if they don't eat everything they can whenever they can, they might miss out and walk away empty.

The truth is that we have the wisdom and ability to listen to our stomachs and resist food when we've had enough. We tend not to believe this, though, because for years we've let diets, food programs, pills, doctors, and magazines tell us what to do. When learning about our hungry/full mechanism, one thing is for sure: with some practice and awareness, we can pinpoint the exact sensation of having enough and walk away feeling satisfied.

I like to compare the hungry/full sensation to a fuel gauge on the dashboard. The empty mark is the starving point, where we feel pain and grumbling in our stomachs. A fourth of a tank is a feeling of hunger where you're ready to eat, but the ravenous sensation of being empty isn't there. This is a good place on the hunger gauge, where you anticipate eating something enjoyable but don't feel so starved that you may binge and overeat.

At the half-tank mark, you may feel that you could eat a bit, but you're not really *hungry*. Sometimes after a large lunch you may still feel about half full when dinnertime rolls around.

This is a time when eating a small amount will satisfy, or you may choose to sow a seed and skip dinner.

At three-fourths of a tank you feel comfortable, but the sensation of fullness hasn't hit. It's that point where you say, "I feel good, and I'll leave room for a small dessert or coffee." After years of either starving myself obsessively and denying hunger or bingeing without any knowledge of true hunger and full sensations, it's liberating to be at three-fourths of a tank and make a conscious decision about how I'll proceed. I can either stuff myself and go beyond the full mark or proceed with caution and confidence and take in a little more food that will leave me satisfied and proud rather than stuffed and sick!

The Hunger Scale

This tool is going to help you avoid eating mindlessly. The more in touch you are with your hunger, the less you need to count calories. Eat only when you're feeling 1, 2, 3 or 4. Put your fork down at 5 or 6, and wait until the next meal or snack. If you're trying to lose weight, stop at 5, the point at which you're eating a little less than your body is burning.

10—Stuffed. You're so full you feel nauseous.

9—Very uncomfortably full. You need to loosen your clothes.

8—Uncomfortably full. You feel bloated.

7—Full. A little bit uncomfortable.

6—Perfectly comfortable. You feel satisfied.

5—Comfortable. You're more or less satisfied but could eat a little more.

4—Slightly uncomfortable. You're just beginning to feel signs of hunger.

3—Uncomfortably hungry. Your stomach is rumbling.

2—Very uncomfortable. You feel irritable and unable to concentrate.

1—Weak and lightheaded. Your stomach acid is churning.[3]

In *Best Life Diet: The Basics,* Bob Greene shares his view of the hunger scale. He mentions that the more aware we are of our hunger, the less we need to resort to old behaviors such as counting calories and restricting foods.

The hungry/full mechanism in our bodies wants to be acknowledged and heeded. God created a miraculous digestive system, and when we abuse this design by regularly overeating, denying our true hunger and starving, or throwing up what we've ingested, the system and fuel tanks in our bodies eventually malfunction. I've often wondered how I got so off-track with food. In thinking about it, I've realized that it's a subtle yet powerful nag from what's normal to an unhealthy acceptance of abnormal.

Perhaps you grew up in a large family, and you had to fight to get enough food. You gobbled yours up quickly so you could grab seconds before the food was eaten by your siblings. Years later, you still gobble up food, just so you won't be left out.

Many of you may have been taught that you must always clean your plate. "There are people starving in . . ." Fill in the name of the country your family used. This common cliché serves to make kids feel guilty for not eating everything put in front of them. A saying I repeated to myself often during my healing was "Garbage in the trash can, garbage in my body. I choose the trash can!"

I'm not suggesting you should waste food. I'm merely presenting the truth that your body is not a garbage disposal! If you've had enough to eat and there's still food on your plate, either you can take it off your plate and wrap it up, or you can throw it out. If you eat it to avoid wasting it, you *are* wasting it—inside your body! That doesn't help you or starving children.

I shared the following story with a group of women that left them gasping and shaking their heads. I explained that I was asked to bring a dessert to a meeting I was scheduled to attend. I stopped and bought a beautiful spice cake at a bakery to take with me. After the meeting, half the cake was left, so I brought it home. The next day I enjoyed a piece of cake. No one else in my house seemed to want any, so I threw out the cake. "What?" women lamented when I shared this account. "I would have eaten the whole cake!" I knew I didn't want the cake sitting around for days with no one else interested in it, so I simply tossed it and never thought of it again. This may seem dramatic, but to a compulsive eater there's freedom that comes from learning to throw food away.

If you find that guilt is still lingering inside, countless shelters and food pantries are located in nearly every town and city in the country that distribute food to needy people. Any local church can direct you to an organization near you that would welcome your donations. This is a tangible way you can help people who don't have food rather than eating past full yourself because you feel guilty about wasting food.

This also applies to restaurants or parties where food is served according to someone else's determination of what a serving should be. Just because it's served to you doesn't mean you have to eat it all. There's freedom in wrapping up the remainder of a dish you enjoyed eating at a restaurant and taking it home to have for lunch the next day. Even if you eat it later that night—if you're hungry—it's a step in the right direction not to feel compelled to eat it all if you're comfortably full.

Many people have shared with me that they felt food was a control mechanism their parents or grandparents used. If this was the case in your life, you may have learned at an early age to stop listening to hunger and merely respond to an adult's commands. "Eat, eat! I made this dish for you, so you're going to eat it!"

On the other hand, some parents strictly forbid certain foods; thus, a control game is set up—usually resulting in rebellion and overuse of the exact foods forbidden. "If you eat that brownie, you'll get spanked! You know you're not allowed to eat sugar!"

When I was growing up, a girlfriend of mine wasn't allowed to eat anything with sugar in it. She also wasn't allowed white bread, chips, or any of the treats kids usually love. I remember her coming to my house after school and making four slices of white toast soaked in butter and sugar. At lunch she traded her nutritious sandwich for a Twinkie or cookies. This went on for years. The more her mother tried to control her eating, the more she went in the opposite direction. The best wisdom we can use and pass on to our children regarding eating habits is to listen to our stomachs and stop when satisfied. If she had not been tortured about it, I believe my girlfriend would have enjoyed her nutritious food. I certainly did. She traded with me daily for the Twinkies!

AN ANOREXIC'S VIEW OF HUNGER

If you're struggling with anorexia or blatant forms of starvation, *hunger* is the feeling you pursue. If you don't feel hungry—for some that means hungry to the point of feeling weak or dizzy—you feel guilty and anxiously await those welcome stomach pains.

I used to love to see how little I could get away with eating while at the same time preparing homemade breads, desserts, and meals that I wouldn't touch. I studied cookbooks and recipes and secretly *thought* about food all the time—yet denied my own true hunger by feeding my body small amounts of regimented foods. Hunger became my warped sense of security. If I was hungry, I knew I was losing weight, and losing weight meant

I was doing something good. The love I felt toward hunger was so deeply entrenched in me that when I started to gain some much-needed weight, my entire security system was stripped, sending me into a tailspin of destructive behavior.

Anorexics feel true hunger but deny their bodies the satisfaction of the hunger. Their bodies literally begin to deplete themselves, damaging tissues and organs, gums, teeth, and the reproductive system.

As I was writing this book, I stumbled upon a web site called ProAnorexia. My mouth hung open in disbelief as I read the comments and tips this writer offered. She listed a full page of distorted opinions about hunger and a page of insider tips to continue a starvation plan. The header on her web site stated, "Hunger hurts, but starvation works." I felt as if I were reading lies straight from the pit of hell. These lies twisted, distorted, and mangled the truth of God's plan for hunger in our lives. As a former anorexic thinker myself, I understand the temptation to believe these damaging insults to truth.

If you struggle with this hunger game, please know that you're not alone. A lot of people don't understand this strange way of viewing hunger, but I do. Now that I'm free from the need for constant hunger, I realize that I was clinging to an illusion of truth that whispered that losing weight and staying thinner than anyone else around me was my crowning glory. After experiencing a revelation of Jesus' commitment to truth in my life, I realized that my body isn't the enemy. Food isn't the enemy. Hunger is not a combative friend.

This isn't another diet or program that may help for a while and then fail in the long run. You're learning about a new, free way of life. Anything that's life-changing takes some time. It has taken a while to develop your distorted relationship with food, so take a deep breath, smile at yourself, and thank God that He's right here to help you understand your hunger, and begin making the right choices regarding it.

THE DEPRIVAL/BINGE CYCLE

What is it about denying ourselves something that makes us want to have it all the more? You may not believe this, but I didn't allow myself to eat sugar, or anything with sugar in it, for seven years. I was terrified that if I ate sugar in any shape or form I would instantly gain weight and fall into out-of-control behavior. Instead, I struggled with overeating foods like low-fat cottage cheese, apples, and dry shredded wheat.

Yes, you can overeat any kind of food, and even though it may be healthful "diet food," you're still eating it gluttonously and feeling awful when you're finished.

Depriving yourself of a variety of foods that you would like to eat sets up what I call the deprival/binge cycle. When you follow a regimented, dictated guideline regarding everything you put into your mouth, eventually you'll snap and binge on all the foods you've felt deprived of. Here's an example: You feel displeased with your body, so you begin a diet. After a few days, weeks, or months of following a restricted food plan, perhaps you've lost some weight, or you're just tired of the diet. As you begin to eat on your own again, you stuff in anything that looks appealing, because you know that when this cycle of bingeing is over, you'll have to deny yourself that food again.

Depriving yourself manifests in two ways. First is a deprival of food in general. Some people refuse to eat anything during the day, and then they have a small meal or nibble on something at night. This starvation may continue for some time until the person gets sick of depriving himself or herself. The floodgates are then opened, and a full-blown binge takes place. You may not see a big change in this person's weight—because the cycles balance themselves. To the extreme, an anorexic may continue this starvation cycle, fearful that eating food in any amount will cause weight gain.

The second type of deprival is one that dictates that certain foods are forbidden. Eating these foods is a no-no and cannot be allowed—foods such as donuts, bread, cookies, ice cream, fries, pizza, pasta, and so on.

At one point in my life I had such a restricted diet that I barely ate anything other than fruit, vegetables, and fish. You may think this sounds healthful, but our bodies need a variety of foods to function properly. After a couple months of such restricted eating, my gums had sores on them, I was severely constipated, and my kidneys were showing signs of damage. As I sat in the doctor's office for a routine check-up, I shared with him that I hadn't had a normal bowel movement for almost five weeks. He knew that I had suffered from anorexia years ago, and his words burned in my heart: "Gari, you're severely harming your body, and it has to stop!"

How could I be so stupid? I wondered. It was because of anorexia that I chose Jesus over suicide many years ago. I had fallen back into the very pit I was rescued from. Even though I had healed immensely from my original state of anorexia to live a happy, full life—I gave birth to my two daughters during this period—I was still functioning with my mind set on deprival. There are many rules and regulations to be obeyed once one adopts this mind-set:

- Order only salads without dressing when eating with others. (You then binge later, when alone.)
- Never eat sweets except during a binge.
- Never allow yourself little things such as butter on bread or sugar in tea.

- Buy ice cream for the kids but not for yourself. (You then gorge on their leftovers or eat from the carton late at night.)

Sometimes we don't realize that we're depriving ourselves of the normal enjoyment of food that leads to an ugly binge of the very foods we feel deprived of.

In her book *Fed Up*, Wendy Oliver Pratt cites research done on the deprival/binge cycle:

> Dieters who think they've eaten "bad" high-calorie foods will continue to binge on other "bad" foods at hand—even if the food that began the binge was really low in calories. Why? Because dieting makes forbidden foods seem compelling and trains you to believe that you have no will power in the absence of external controls. The result: when you finally rebel against these external controls, and give in to the urge to eat "bad" foods, you eat until you are sickened, both physically and emotionally, by your bingeing.[4]

Doesn't it make sense? The more you deprive yourself of the natural desire to eat a variety of foods, the more obsessed and compulsive you'll be about eating them. Whether you actually go through with a binge or just think about food obsessively, the cycle is in motion.

To further illustrate this point, picture a little girl walking home from school every day with her mother. They walk past a beautiful, lush park. It has a set of swings, a slide, a merry-go-round, a sandbox, and a large tree house for the children.

The little girl innocently asks her mom if she can spend some time playing at the park. Her mother pulls the little girl to her and looks into her face. She tells her that although the park looks inviting and is open to everyone, she isn't allowed to play there. The little girl questions the mother's verdict. "Mommy, why can't I play there? I see my friends playing there. I won't stay for long!"

Her mother grabs her hand and hastily pulls her along the sidewalk, away from the park. She can hear her mother mumbling some vague reasons why it isn't good for her to play there. "You might slip and get hurt," and "You might like it so much there that you'll never return home."

The little girl listens to her mother's mumbling and thinks how silly it seems. Yet she obeys the rule she has been given and returns home.

The next day she walks home by herself. As she passes the park she remembers that she's not allowed to play there. Her friends shout out to her from the park: "Come on! Come join us!"

"No," she replies. "I can't play there. Thanks anyway."

The following day as she approaches the park, she begins to think, *Maybe I can just swing really quickly and go down the slide once. My mom won't know, and I'll hurry home afterward.*

Each day she spends a little more time in the forbidden park. She now lies to her mother and gets home later. She finds herself constantly thinking about the park and dreams of ways to spend time there without getting caught. One day she actually skips school and spends the entire day in the park, hiding out. She's scared that someone will catch her yet feels compelled to be there. She realizes that she isn't even enjoying the time she spends in the park. It has become an obsession. Yet because of the silly, unrealistic rule that initially forbade her the pleasure of the park, she was overcome with finding ways to invade that forbidden territory.

Where do we get our rules and regulations regarding food? Is there someone in your life—or is it you—who dictates stringent regulations on what you're allowed to eat, even though the regulations make no sense? There's no reason you can't enjoy the foods you want to eat. The problem isn't what you choose to eat—it's eating gluttonously. It's as if the food police handcuffed us to a lie that makes us want to rebel. Thus, a binge cycle begins.

After not allowing myself anything sweet for seven years, I was a little hesitant to let go of the lie that was controlling me. I learned that what I clung to as truth was simply a fearful restriction, and I began to let go of my deprival mentality.

There are two ways I believe you can blast this mentality from your heart.

1. Let go of the good food/bad food list. If you ask people who have suffered from disordered eating, I think it would be unanimous that, in their minds, they believe that certain foods are good and certain foods are bad. The intensity and range of these beliefs vary. Compulsive overeaters may eat any kind of food they want to, but mentally they hate themselves and feel they've blown it when they eat foods from the "bad" list. An anorexic won't touch certain foods for fear they're too fattening, and a bulimic will usually binge on the foods that are on the bad list, then try to get rid of what he or she ate by throwing up or taking laxatives. The bad list becomes the judge in a struggle for good behavior with food.

For me, the list of bad foods was endless. I didn't allow myself sweets of any kind, butter, pizza, pasta, bread, or any kind of fast food item for years. I prepared meals for my family and never allowed myself to touch them. I felt I wasn't allowed to enjoy normal foods. That kind of normal eating was okay for others, but not for me.

Geneen Roth made me laugh when she described this phenomenon in her life. She explained that after feeling bound to the rules and regulations of diets, she finally came to the point at which she threw it all aside and decided to eat whatever she wanted. The thing she really wanted to eat—but hadn't allowed herself to for years—was chocolate chip cookie dough. She decided that if she wanted chocolate chip cookie dough for breakfast, lunch, and dinner, then so be it! After eating cookie dough for a while, the thrill wore off, and she desired a variety of other foods that filled and satisfied her.

When I talk about eating whatever you want in a reasonable, adequate quantity, people begin to feel afraid. They fear that if they allow themselves the freedom to eat what they want, they'll gobble up not only that particular food but also most everything else in the refrigerator! The truth is—when you allow yourself to eat what you desire, the exact opposite begins to occur. When you eat what you really want to eat, you'll be amazed that it doesn't take much to make you feel full and satisfied. And the best part is that you don't end up feeling cheated and pressed to rebel.

If your family is having pie for dessert and you want some, sit down like a normal human being, cut yourself a small piece, and enjoy it! It sure beats sneaking around later with your spoon in the pie pan, scooping up bites that cause you to feel guilty. The key to eating what you want is to listen to your stomach and stop when you're full. When you binge, it's usually on foods you don't ordinarily allow yourself to eat. Most people binge on sweets, chips, or fast-food items, stuffing in as much as they can, because they know tomorrow they won't allow themselves to eat that kind of food.

Listen to this truth: You can eat any kind of food in adequate, normal amounts, stop when you're full, and maintain or actually lose weight. I was amazed to realize that I could enjoy a small dish of ice cream every night after dinner without gaining a pound. A whole new world opened up to me as I allowed myself to eat whatever I really wanted to eat. As I began to eat from desire rather than fear, I realized that I enjoy healthful foods, but I'm free to choose what I want to eat.

2. Apply the principle of sowing seeds to the deprival/binge mentality. As mentioned in chapter two, sowing seeds to God regarding your eating is an act of worship in which you choose the truth over lies that have tainted your relationship with food. When caught in the deprival/binge mentality, you tell yourself you can't have certain foods because they're bad. Typically, each time you eat them—or binge them—you heap a load of condemnation on yourself. You beat yourself up because of your choices. To apply seed-sowing in this area, you must determine to retrain your thought patterns. When faced with a food you believe you shouldn't eat, instead of listening to the "good food/bad food" lie, pray, using this scripture as a guide:

> The kingdom of God is not eating or drinking, but righteousness and peace and joy in the Holy Spirit (*Romans 14:17*).

God wants to fill you with peace and joy regarding your choices with food. If we counted the hours in a week that we spend laboring over, restricting, and condemning our eating patterns, it would stand as an embarrassing trophy of defeat. In the midst of this depressing cycle, God whispers an offer of peace. When faced with the choice to overeat beyond what makes you feel full, or the need to limit foods you eat only to binge on them secretly later, talk back to the lie that promises fulfillment in food. Sow a seed to God by reciting His promises to you.

I recited this scripture as I stood in front of the kitchen cabinet, ready to grab for food I really didn't want to eat: "Then they cried out to the LORD in their trouble; He saved them out of their distresses. He sent His word and healed them, and delivered them from their destructions" (Psalm 107:19-20).

To retrain your mind you will want to arm yourself with the right tools. Two of the most potent tools to apply in your mental seed-sowing are scriptures and phrases. Use scriptures you see throughout this book and those that God sheds light on as you comb through your Bible. Put them on sticky notes, index cards, a journal, or anywhere else you'll have visual access. I put cards up on my cabinets, on my refrigerator, and in my car to remind me that I can choose to sow mental seeds to God regarding my food choices rather than feeling powerless over food.

I also recommend adopting a phrase that will serve as a type of mental ointment in the retraining of your mind. If you're like me, scripture memorization is a bit like studying profusely for a test, only to forget everything you learned when you need to write it on paper! To remedy this situation, I started using a phrase that helped me when I couldn't pull up a scripture from my mind. As I shared earlier, one phrase I used was "I don't do that anymore." I also used the phrase "I'm free to eat like a normal person."

At first I felt like a fake, as if I were trying to brainwash myself. But as I started talking back to the lies that kept popping up into my mind, the lies began to loose their punch. By using many of the scriptures I've shared and simply stating phrases such as "I'm free to sow good seed to God and break my habits" or "I'm making new choices now," my mind began to sense a new season dawning.

I once heard a wise pastor compare our lives to waterskiing. When waterskiing, if you fall, the best thing to do is let go of the rope so you can wait for the boat to come around and then try again. In our lives, if something isn't working and is actually dragging us down, we must let go of the rope and start on a new course. If you hang on to the rope, you'll get dragged through the water. Why do that when you can let go and start over? It's time to let go of the good food/bad food list and the deprival/binge mentality that has led you through threatening waters. When you let go, you're free to learn about true hunger.

Personal Morsels

In this chapter we talked about physical hunger, spiritual hunger, and emotional hunger. How well are you satisfying these three types of hunger in your life? Is there one area that feels more in sync than the others?

_____

_____

_____

_____

_____

_____

_____

_____

Read Hosea 11:4, and personalize it here.

_____

_____

_____

_____

_____

_____

_____

_____

How does Hosea 11:4 compare to Matthew 11:29-30, in which Jesus explains that His yoke is easy and His load is light?

_____

_____

_____

_____

_____

_____

_____

_____

_____

Use the space below to draw your circle diagrams and record your eating patterns for a few consecutive days. Do you see any surprises?

What foods are on your "good food/bad food" list? Why are they there?

Good Foods   **Bad Foods**

_____

_____

_____

_____

_____

_____

_____

_____

_____

_____

FOUR

Do You Dare Eat What Is Set Before You?

Yesterday I heard a commercial on the radio that had me shaking my head. The advertisement claimed that all we need do to be healthy, lose weight, and feel great is to eat as Jesus ate back when He walked the earth. They provide a list of what they assume He ate and invite others to buy the book and learn the secrets.

Although I'm certain Jesus ate well and in moderation, the people of that day who ate the same basic diet as Jesus still had serious health issues. Keeping in mind Jesus' healing ministry, if there was a particular food plan that was best for humanity, don't you think He would have let us in on it?

Diane Hampton shares her insight on this in *The Diet Alternative* as she relates scripture in Luke to God's invitation to "eat what is set before you."[1]

As Jesus sent seventy disciples out to minister two by two, His instructions were precise and intentional:

> Whatever house you enter, first say, "Peace be to this house." And if a man of peace is there, your peace will rest upon him; but if not, it will return to you. And stay in that house, eating and drinking what they give you; for the laborer is worthy of his wages. . . . And whatever city you enter, and they receive you, eat what is set before you (*Luke 10:5-8*).

Jesus told them in so many words not to worry about what they were eating. The society we live in sends the opposite message. It says, "Worry intensely about what you eat. Live in fear, guilt, and condemnation about all your behaviors with food." What a contrast to Jesus' instructions simply to eat what's set before you!

PAUL'S WORDS OF WISDOM REGARDING FOOD

In his letters to the people living in Corinth, Paul speaks boldly about the role of food in our lives. He starts out by saying, "All things are lawful for me, but not all things are profitable. All things are lawful for me, but *I will not be mastered by anything.* Food is for the stomach, and the stomach is for food; but God will do away with both of them" (1 Corinthians 6:12-13, emphasis added).

If you have a pen or highlighter handy, please underline the phrase "I will not be mastered by anything." Paul knew that food itself wasn't the issue but rather being mastered by its power over our lives. He puts it in perspective by then explaining that food is for the stomach, and the stomach is for food, and in the end God does away with them both. The time, energy, and emotion we twist around food really take us nowhere.

Yet for all his advice about food, Paul has an understanding of the intensity of our plight. Later in his letter to the Corinthians, while talking about freedom and worshiping one God alone, he states, "However, not all men have this knowledge; but some, being accustomed to the idol until now, *eat food* as if it were sacrificed to an idol; and their conscience being weak is defiled. But food will not commend us to God; we are neither the worse if we do not eat, nor the better if we do eat" (1 Corinthians 8:7-8, emphasis added).

Are you accustomed to the idol of food worship? Are you eating food—or starving and purging—as if sacrificing to a foreign god?

This may seem extreme, but when we're deep in the throes of a binge, purge, or starvation cycle, common sense is lost, and we robotically cling to the bizarre behavior we hate. It's as though we lay the food on an altar—or countertop or table—and worship the momentary taste or the way it makes us feel.

In Christian circles we tend to isolate the word *idol*, pushing it to the pages of Old Testament golden calves and graven images. It's hard to imagine that gluttonous eating, or obsession with body weight, can be idolatrous. An idol is a fetish or a false god that takes the place of a holy, grace-filled God.

Real versus counterfeit.

Fake versus authentic.

If we're honest with ourselves, we have to admit that there are many things that rise up as idols in our lives. Some have their reign over particular seasons and eventually lose their luster.

I remember when I first started dating my husband, Bobby. He was a baseball star, handsome, wonderful, perfect. You get the picture. I was completely overtaken by his power in my life. If he called, I was happy. If he had a bad game playing shortstop for our college team, I was sad. His outlook and actions dictated my happiness. Some might say that this is normal in the early glow of a relationship, and I agree. But after a while, I remember thinking that I had made him something he was never meant to be in my life: a mini-god. I shifted focus and remained deeply in love with him, but I transferred that unhealthy dependence back onto the only one worthy of that kind of devotion—my Lord Jesus.

Some have made a job their idol. Even good things like family, loving our children, or our health can become idols when they push God off the throne to magnify themselves.

Let's look at some of the ways we succumb to idol worship when it comes to food.

This list may touch a defensive nerve. You may feel more like a victim than a perpetrator of idol worship. But consider

---

Characteristics of Worshiping Food as an Idol

- Eating consistently with no connection to body hunger
- Bingeing compulsively
- Lying about eating habits
- Causing oneself to throw up or otherwise eliminate what's been ingested
- Constantly restating lies that govern our minds and processing ability:

    I'll always be fat.

    I don't deserve to feel good about my weight and body.

    I have no self-discipline.

    I must remain in a constant state of control.

    This is my body, and I'll do with it as I please!

---

that idol worship is the consumption of thought, action, and belief in anything other than the true God.

I asked myself these questions when I considered my battle with food and idol worship:

1. *Do I consume food as if I'm in communion with a force I can't control?* This is in conflict with being led and filled by the Holy Spirit. See Romans 8:10-11.

2. *Do I think of food and dieting in an abnormal way?* This conflicts with God's assurance that my mind and my flesh, with their passions and desires, have been crucified with Christ. See Galatians 5:24-25.

3. *Do I rebelliously believe that this is my body, and I'll do with it as I please?* This conflicts with 1 Corinthians 6:19-20, which states that my body is the home of the Holy Spirit, and I am not my own. I've been bought with a price—Christ's death.

When we acknowledge the ways in which we've made food an idol, we're free to change our rituals and behaviors.

In Judges 6, Gideon—an insecure, unlikely, hand-picked leader chosen by God—smashed the false idols of Baal in his community, because he was so sure of God's presence and strength.

> Now the same night it came about that the LORD said to him, "Take your father's bull, and a second bull seven years old, and pull down the altar of Baal which belongs to your father, and cut down the Asherah [wooden symbol of a female deity] that is beside it; and build an altar to the LORD your God *on top of this stronghold* in an orderly manner, and take a second bull and offer a burnt offering with the wood of the Asherah which you shall cut down" (*Judges 6:25-26, emphasis added*).

God told Gideon to go after the false gods of his father. That's enough to leave anyone shaking in his or her boots. But the most powerful part of this scripture is that God didn't just want the false idols torn down—He instructed Gideon to build an altar to Him right on top of the former idol! In other words, what was once an idol for destruction and lies would become an altar of hope to the living God—a place for true communication, authenticity, and shame-free living.

Although it may seem easier to crush statues and physical altars than to put away the idols we've created in our minds and habits, the same power and assurance Gideon had are available to us.

Was he afraid? Yes—just as we may be afraid to attack our idols for fear that we may not have the strength to overcome them.

Did Gideon fear a possible fall-out after he took his stand? Surely—just as we may struggle with the uncertainty of living a new life free of our idols' hold.

Was it worth it? Absolutely—just as the new freedom you'll find will replace the bankruptcy you've endured with food.

Paul explains that some of us are accustomed to the idol, indicating that the blind acceptance of our habits has led to our continued act of destructive worship. We were created to worship and enjoy our God, and food was created for fuel, nourishment, and community. In this clear picture there's no room for idol worship.

ARE DESSERTS THE EVIL EMPIRE?

As mentioned earlier, restricting foods typically leads to the desire to binge on them. Sweets are not the problem, but society has played on our weakness to make us believe they are. Commercials showing desperate women saying, "Chocolate is sinfully delicious!" make us feel that we're doing something wrong when we enjoy dessert. Eating sweets while paying attention to the hungry/full mechanism we've been created with is one of the joys of being human.

You may have noticed that sweets are mentioned throughout the Bible. Vines, figs, pomegranates, and honey are repeatedly mentioned in Scripture. As a matter of fact, in a prophecy foretelling Jesus' life, Isaiah mentions that Jesus will eat curds and honey. Basically, Isaiah is referring to butter and honey, making Jesus' diet sound more like Southern cooking than Jewish cuisine!

I love to order dessert when I'm with my family or friends and relish the sweet taste. I typically want only a few bites to feel satisfied, and I don't feel cheated or punished for enjoying it.

My daughter Ally and I have some fun habits when it comes to ice cream. We like to sit together, spoons in hand, and eat from the carton. We have great conversation as we eat, and after several bites we're satisfied. It's really more about the ritual than the ice cream, but the ice cream makes it fun. I have Girl Scout cookies (Thin Mints) that have taken up space in my refrigerator for five months, and I may end up throwing them out if they don't get eaten soon. One of my friends was appalled when I shared this with her. She said, "I can't have those things in my house. They'd be gone in one sitting. How do you do it?"

I replied, "I'm free to eat them or not. I don't really think about it!" In all fairness, I remember a time when I would have thought about those cookies constantly. But my new life and relationship with food don't accept that behavior anymore.

My friend smiled at me and shook her head and mumbled, "It must be nice to be so free."

You have no idea, I said to myself. *You have no idea.*

EATING AS COMMUNITY BEHAVIOR

One thing you can be certain of is that God is a God of community. He believes in living in community rather than isolation. As a matter of fact, even before the creation of earth, God the Father lived in community with His Son and the Holy Spirit. See Genesis 3.

It's no surprise that His authentic blueprint for the role of food in community is the complete opposite of disordered eating. God's plan uses food to bring people together for conversation and interaction. Disordered eating encourages eating in secrecy and isolation. God loves to see His people enjoy the fruit of His creation, and that includes the act of eating with others for enjoyment.

Often our schedules dictate that we eat alone or on the run, but eating with family and friends, even if it's just mac and cheese or a sandwich, is typically more enjoyable.

Consider the relationship Jesus had with His friends Martha, Mary, and Lazarus. He frequently ate meals with them, and their friendship and intimacy grew. See Luke 16.

When Jesus met Zaccheus—a rich, hated tax-collector who had to go tree-climbing to see Jesus over the crowd—the first thing Jesus said to him was "Come down out of the tree. I'm coming to dinner!" See Luke 19.

At a blow-out wedding that Jesus attended with his family and friends in Cana, the wine was quickly consumed, and the bride and groom were faced with embarrassment. But Jesus restored it to a successful, joyful gathering based on community, food, and drink.

One of the first mentions of fast food is when Jesus and His disciples were walking through fields of grain as their stomachs began to rumble. They ate the heads of grain right off the stalks as they walked, much to the distaste of the Pharisees, who criticized them for picking grain on the Sabbath. Jesus and His crew ate the grain together as they traveled, no doubt smirking at the Pharisees' lack of understanding.

Finally, the Lord chose a last supper with His closest friends to share some of the most profound truths found in the Bible. See John 13.

God values community eating. Whether it's dinner out with friends, eating together as a family, or dining at parties or gatherings, the act of sharing a meal diminishes the power of hidden behavior with food.

A DAY IN THE LIFE OF A FREE PERSON

One night as I was preparing to teach a Truly Fed class, a dear woman named Becky came up to me holding a typewritten page. She said, "Remember how you mentioned writing down our dream of what it would be like to live free from disordered eating? Well, here's mine." Our entire class enjoyed her insight and hope. I hope you do too.

I wake up with a sense of hope as I face the day. I shower, and my shape or size, wrinkles or sags, age spots or scars don't even cross my mind as I'm toweling off in front of the bathroom mirror. I go to the closet, and since everything is the same size, I don't have to try on numerous items to see what fits this month. It takes me far less time to get dressed, because I also don't have to decide which pieces of clothing make me look fat, which ones make me look bottom heavy or top heavy or square or round or old and lumpy.

I eat breakfast without guilt and totally savor my coffee. As I go about my morning, I don't give food a thought. About 10:30 someone brings in donuts. Not a problem! I can have one or not. I decide to take one, but after two bites, it's too sweet to finish, and I throw it away and couldn't care less.

I make myself a sandwich for lunch, and, yes, it's more carbohydrates for the day, but I'm out of chicken and tuna makings. I don't stress; peanut butter and jelly will work just fine. Every bite is a delight.

About mid-afternoon my husband calls. Some friends want to meet us for dinner at a buffet. What fun! They're great friends, delightful to be with, and food is just food. We spend so much time laughing and talking that the buffet is not "calling my name." The salad makings are terrific, and who has time for seconds? I might miss some of this conversation.

I've spent a day free of former temptations and the possibilities of grossly overeating. I'm truly fed and truly free—and I look forward to a new day tomorrow.

This isn't a fantasy—a dream reserved only for women blessed with high metabolism and perfect thighs. It's God's design for all of us. *We can be truly fed and free.* This is God's purpose, intention, and desire.

Personal Morsels

In this chapter a woman shared what a day in the life of a free person looks like. What would this kind of day look like to you? Write your thoughts here.

Read Habakkuk 2:2-3, and write it out below.

This scripture talks about recording the vision. In what way is the day you just described your vision of a different kind of life?

_____

_____

_____

_____

_____

_____

_____

_____

_____

_____

In this scripture God says to wait for the vision, though it may tarry, because it still hastens toward the goal. How does this encourage you?

_____

_____

_____

_____

_____

_____

_____

_____

_____

FIVE

That Was Then—This Is Now

Behold, the former things have come to pass, Now I declare new things; Before they spring forth I proclaim them to you *(Isaiah 42:9)*.

The mountains echoed the glory of a summer day in Colorado. Scanning the green meadow before me and the towering pine trees behind me, I soaked in the moment. My family had gathered for a July 4 celebration on the land my grandparents passed down to us. More than thirty people from across the country had flown in for the weeklong getaway. My sister had hired a small band to play for our gathering. The band was set up in a covered shed that was filled with dirt and a few pesky piles of old cow manure.

I danced with friends and family for hours, and during that time I pondered the joy of healing in our lives. I looked at my mom's infectious smile, savored my brother's expectant wife's belly, and kicked up my boots with my arm around my sister's shoulder. If you had told me thirty years earlier that I would take part in a celebration such as this, I would have smirked at the impossibility of its ever happening. My childhood was scarred by dark, damaging events. Even today, all these years later, certain memories make my heart ache.

My dad was a young, handsome bank president, and my mom was a beauty queen from Maryland. They had three children and a lovely home but a troubled marriage. On a late summer night in July, my dad was driving home from a bank party when his car swerved off the road and tumbled down an embankment. The accident left him paralyzed from the neck down.

My mom turned to alcohol to numb the pain of our family's tragedy. Our family spiraled into chaos and a lingering depression. I was nine years old at the time of my dad's accident.

My sister was six, and my little brother was a thumb-sucking three years old. The shocking necessity of becoming adult-like at such an early age was a reality I didn't understand.

I remember turning to food occasionally to soothe my fear and unhappiness. Chips, pastries, Twinkies, and cupcakes were my favorites. Once as I sat alone with a bag of chips, I uttered the words "This food will never disappoint me or hurt me." Because of an active sports lifestyle, I didn't struggle with weight issues until I was older, but I felt as if food were an intimate ally in my lonely world.

As I grew older, my relationship with food became more and more unhealthy. Eating was a secret tryst I cherished as I sneaked out for fast food or binged privately in my bedroom. Food was my friend and confidant. But as I began to put on weight in college, it soon became a bond I hated but was incapable of escaping.

When I began strict dieting, I substituted one obsession for another. I loved losing weight and the attention I received, but when I started to regain pounds I really needed to regain, the cycle of self-hatred began again.

I'm often struck by the way we internalize our past and the effect that has on our relationship with food. One woman who struggles with being overweight shared that when she was young a trusted pastor was sexually inappropriate toward her, and afterward he offered her bread with butter and sugar on it. She wept as she shared, "To this day, those are the foods that have caused me trouble!"

Another woman shared that her overbearing mother constantly forced food on her during her childhood, and there were other issues with her mother as well. When she became an adult, she viewed food as something she could control, and she refused to eat enough to sustain a normal body weight. As she withered away to a dangerously low body weight, she was exhilarated to smirk in the face of a controlling parent and ultimately say, "You can't make me!"

Through the experiences in my own life and the stories I've heard from the men and women I've enjoyed knowing, the common thread that knits our stories together seems to be that something in the past has pushed us toward our unhealthy relationships with food. Not everyone can trace the beginnings of his or her destructive relationship with food, but most people seem to find a connection.

I often ask people to sit quietly for a few minutes and pray for the Holy Spirit to reveal to them at what point in their lives their obsession with food began.

Take a few minutes to think about this now. Maybe it didn't begin when you were a child; maybe there was a slow-moving process from normalcy to obsession that began after you reached adulthood. As you reflect on the starting point in these few minutes, write down your thoughts.

_____

_____

_____

_____

_____

_____

_____

_____

_____

_____

Recognizing the starting points of disordered eating can lead us to a place of healing and revelation—a place at which we can begin to mark the end of compulsion with food.

BREAKING GENERATIONAL CYCLES

If we were to lay out the history of most families, we would typically see cycles of behaviors that are passed down from generation to generation. Some behaviors are good and nurturing, while others are destructive and damaging. Cycles of sexual, physical, and verbal abuse; alcoholism; drug addiction; fear; control; and rage are often passed from parent to child within a family.

Children often repeat in adulthood what they learned from observing their parents' behaviors. As the parent of three children, I realize how fragile and precious a child's personality is. It breaks my heart to realize that as an imperfect human parent, some of my words, actions, and habits hurt my children, although my intent is to love and encourage them. It wasn't until I was an adult, trying to figure out how my relationship with food got so mangled, that I realized that some of my behavior had been passed down through generations.

I adored my grandfather. He was loving and funny, and made me feel as if I were the most important person in the world to him. He was overweight, and I remember as a kid how I grabbed onto his big belly when he and I fought waves in the ocean. Each summer my siblings and I stayed with our grandparents for a month, and I remember hearing my grandfather get up several times throughout the night to go to the kitchen. I could hear the refrigerator creak open, then the spoons being rattled in the drawer. He was eating ice cream or any other sweet he could find as the night ticked away. My grandmother scolded him repeatedly and even tried to hide the sweets, but he pursued those late-night snacks relentlessly.

He often tried to lose weight. Once he lost fifty pounds by eliminating solid foods—drinking a solution his doctor recommended and receiving B-6 shots every week. He looked like a different man for a time, but he soon regained all the weight when he resumed normal eating. Later in life he struggled with diabetes and ended up dying from a heart attack. He was a wonderful yet plagued man. Food was both his friend and his enemy.

As I reflect on my grandfather's tortured relationship with food, I see that my former behavior resembled his. I, too, ate when I wasn't hungry, ate in secret, dieted to extremes, and felt an unhealthy bondage to food.

Let me give you another example of a generational cycle. My husband, Bobby, was a professional baseball player. He played professionally for ten years, most of them for the New York Yankees. The lifestyle of a major-league player puts temptations before him similar to the temptations of a diabetic in a candy shop. As a Christian ballplayer, my husband stood for marriage and morality. But as his career began to wane, he reverted to old, dangerous behaviors to receive attention and stoke the ego that was now suffering. Women played a part in his fall, and his life came to a crashing halt when he told me about the putrid skeletons in his closet. Our marriage almost didn't make it, and if not for the radical healing and grace of God, I'm certain we wouldn't be together. God not only cleaned out my husband's filthy closet—He also repainted it and put it in order.

As we tried to piece together our shattered marriage many years ago, we noticed a pattern. Both of us had fathers who were unfaithful to our mothers. There was a distinct cycle of trust abuse in our fathers' lives that seemed to be passed down to the next generation. No one ever really dealt with the problem; it was shoved out of sight—like an elephant trying to hide in a pantry.

During this painful time, Bobby and I said, "No more! We will not pass this cycle down to our son. It stops now!" We prayerfully addressed his father's behavior and the damage it had done. My father has lived for almost 40 years in a wheelchair. The night of the accident that left him a quadriplegic, he had been with another woman. He has had to live with the tragic "what-ifs" that followed the poor choices he made.

We prayed fervently for the power of this cycle to be broken in our family once and for all, that the cycle would be replaced by God's wisdom and strength. We prayed these 1 Corinthians words to solidify the importance of purity: "Flee immorality. Every other sin that a man commits is outside the body, but an immoral man sins against his own body. . . . You have been bought with a price: therefore glorify God in your body" (1 Corinthians 6:18, 20).

As our son grew into his late teen years, we shared this story with him and talked often about the essence of purity and devotion in marriage and manhood. We'll continue these conversations when he marries, and my husband hopes to provide the model of a man who walks with God.

Someone once said we're only as sick as our secrets. In the case of generational cycles, family secrets can snuff out the life of freedom that God intends for us. Breaking generational patterns of destructive behavior not only changes our lives but also changes the lives of our children. Both of our daughters have attended Truly Fed classes and seek God's wisdom, discipline, and delight in their view of food. When I began to heal in this area, I prayed blessing and freedom over my young children regarding food. My girls are in their twenties now, and I continue to pray that through effort and awareness they'll have healthy self-images.

BREAKING GENERATIONAL CYCLES

I've recognized four steps that I believe are necessary in moving toward a new life and healing.

Acknowledge the past, and name specific people and events that have caused anguish, perpetuating a negative generational cycle.

Forgive your past so it doesn't dictate your future.

Redefine and recreate who you will be with food or other damaging cycles that you want to break in your life.

Seal your healing. Mark it as a monument in your life—a time you know you've had an encounter with God.

ACKNOWLEDGE THE PAST

To acknowledge the past, you must face the fact that you've been damaged, and that includes acknowledging the people or events that contributed to your distortion of truth. Some people have no problem putting the pieces of the puzzle together that led to pain in their lives. Others, though, try to excuse or minimize the actions that created chaos.

In my life, I know my father's car accident and my mother's alcoholism led me to some dark, lonely places. The hateful words I heard exchanged, scenes I witnessed, and the foreboding sense that something was terribly wrong with me made me susceptible to disordered eating. I believed at one time that being a Christian meant I didn't have to bother with examining the past. After all, I'm new in Christ. While that's true, we're products of the people and events that shaped our youth.

We don't have to stay stuck there, but to deny the influence the past has on our outlook and character is like an ostrich burying its head in the sand. To acknowledge the past means looking at it and saying, "I see that the actions of these people or events pushed me toward a distorted way of dealing with my life [food, addictions, and relationships]. By acknowledging these influences, I can become free to deal with them and move beyond their grip."

"Weapons of mass destruction" is a term we've become familiar with over the past decade or so. I would like to introduce "cycles of mass destruction." There are cycles of addiction, control, and abuse that have the power to obliterate the budding self-esteem of children, eroding their belief that they're precious and loved by God. If you recognize a cycle of mass destruction in your past, please acknowledge it. This enables you to move beyond the cycle and break its power over your future.

FORGIVE YOUR PAST

In his book *Healing Is a Choice*, Stephen Arterburn writes, "The lack of forgiveness is a potent internal cocktail that you administer to yourself to your own detriment every day."[1]

Even doctors acknowledge the power of forgiveness and how it affects healthy cardiac functions, blood pressure, and immune systems.

This is nothing new to those of us who know the power of forgiveness presented in the Bible. Both the Old and New Testaments offer repeated accounts in the lives of kings and commoners that reflect the life-giving potential of forgiveness. The essence of the Cross is Jesus' death for the forgiveness of every wrong I'll ever do or even think about doing. Forgiveness is truly essential in a fallen, broken world.

So why is it so hard? Maybe it's because we have to give up the fuel that harbors our pain and justifies poor choices or habits. To forgive means consciously giving up resentments caused by another's actions. Jesus Christ can fill us with the desire and ability to forgive the incidents and people who have hurt us the most. It goes against logic and most of what the world teaches us.

When you forgive the people and the past that haunt you, something unexplainable begins to develop inside. It may be a desire to pray for the very person who damaged you. It may be a desire to minister and help others who have suffered pain similar to yours. Whatever the case may be, a prayerful decision to forgive the past is the first step.

Please don't confuse forgiveness with endorsing or agreeing with harmful behavior. If you forgive a parent who abused you verbally and physically, you aren't saying that what he or she did was acceptable. It wasn't! When you forgive someone, you're saying in essence, "I know I was harmed by your behavior, but I have the love and life of Jesus inside me. His gift frees me to forgive you and to pray that one day you may experience the treasure of Jesus' love in your life too."

The greater the pain and the deeper the scars, the harder it is to comprehend forgiving. A potent scripture says, "Do not be overcome by evil, but overcome evil with good" (Romans 12:21).

Jesus also says, "He who believes in Me, as the Scripture said, 'From his innermost being shall flow rivers of living water'" (John 7:38).

Picture a stream of water. It moves, gleaming with sunlight, splashing trickles of water from place to place. This is what Christ's love and power are inside us—living water! They cleanse us from the need to harbor bitterness and hatred, and we can gleam with joy and hope for a free, abundant life, constantly moving from experience to experience, growing ʿ maturing.

When forgiving your past, it's important that you learn to separate who you are now from the person you were then. Recognize that according to Scripture you're a new, free creation. When memories or incidents occur that spur pain, remind yourself that you don't have to stay chained to the person you were or bitterly resent the past that cripples you. You can choose to look at your life through another lens.

For most of us, going home—or back to people or circumstances that hurt us—can cause a flood of emotion. Many years ago I returned with my three small children to my childhood home in Colorado. I found it amazing that although I was a grown woman, happily married and raising my own kids, sadness seemed to seep through the walls of the house I grew up in. My week there concluded with a huge argument with my mom. In that argument we managed to dredge up hurt from twenty years earlier. I was shocked to realize that by physically being in the place where I grew up, the old fears and insecurities had grown to the point of explosion.

On my long drive home after that visit, I realized that wherever I am, whatever the circumstance, my life is hidden with Christ in God. (See Colossians 3:3.) I don't have to feel trapped and insecure about the person I was, because I have a new nature inside me.

Shortly after that trip I committed my heart to forgiveness. I forgave my mom for the hurt I harbored and asked her to forgive me for the hurt I dispensed too. After years peppered with grace, dinners, kids' ball games, holidays, and the sweet tick of time between us, I can honestly call my mom one of my best friends. She's the one I want to talk to when I'm afraid or need advice about a big decision. I know it doesn't always turn out this way for everyone; sometimes the pain and damage are too great, or the person who hurt you is gone, and you never got the chance to heal the wounds between you. Sometimes it's dangerous to put yourself in the presence of the person who trashed your heart. But even if you have to do it from a safe distance, you can still forgive.

In his book *Wild at Heart*, John Eldredge speaks about the wounds we experience in life—the places of shame, the hurt, and the scars from an imperfect past. He says that God is fiercely committed to us and to the restoration of our hearts. But a wound that goes unacknowledged and unwept is a wound that can't heal. "A wound you've embraced is a wound that cannot heal. A wound you think you deserved is a wound that cannot heal."[2]

If we embrace our wounds—or the cycle passed down to us, thinking we deserved it, or use it as a lifetime excuse for poor choices—we'll never move beyond it. We'll live in the middle of its oozing, infected stench. By choosing to acknowledge it and forgive it, we clean out the wound and move toward freedom.

REDEFINE AND RECREATE

My all-time favorite movie is *Rocky*. I was in high school when I saw it for the first time in the theater. When it came to the part where he boxes for the title, the entire audience was hooting and clapping. We felt like part of his story. He was a washed-up boxer living a seedy life, trying to make ends meet. Working at a meat-packing plant, Rocky used that setting to keep focused on his goals as he boxed slabs of beef with his hands. When he got his shot at the title, he knew it was a setup—an unrealistic slice of cheese dangled before him—but he decided to view it as a chance to redefine himself and recreate his worth and purpose. Maybe that's why *Rocky* has become one of the most loved movies of all times.

We love to see people triumph over struggles and redefine themselves. Why do we think it's only for the movies? We may not win boxing titles through our inner transformations, but it's still worth hooting and cheering about!

As a young woman, I thought I saw my future. I married a first-round draft pick and figured we would have a life of glamour, financial security, and marital bliss. I was terribly wrong. The glamour looked more like chaos as we moved more than forty-seven times in ten years. Although my husband did well financially for a few years, we soon used up our savings after he was relinquished to the minor leagues and I began working full-time as a teacher. As for marital bliss—we worked through some tough years of immature choices and devastating pain. He's my best friend and the one I love living my life with, but many tears were shed in the process.

Redefining and recreating who you are takes guts. It necessitates letting go of patterns of thinking and behavior and moving toward a different vision of who you want to be.

This often plays out in a person's career choices. At one point in my adult life I felt as if God had blessed me as a writer, so I pursued that goal. I naively called the editor of a sports magazine, *Sports Spectrum*, and told him I had a story I wanted to write. Graciously he listened to me without commenting on the fact that I hadn't followed any of the writer's etiquette rules. He told me to write the piece and send it to him and he would let me know. A few months later I received an acceptance letter and began a six-year stint as a sports reporter for that magazine. I had three young children and was following my husband to all ends of the country as a baseball wife, but I had recreated myself as a reporter.

For some reason, career recreations seem easier than heart recreations. To recreate and redefine the new person I wanted to be, including my relationship with food, I asked God to give me His vision for my life. Who did He see me becoming, and how could I use His vision to redefine myself?

God's vision of us holds a few guarantees that are backed up by His character. We will be free (John 8:36), we will have peace (John 14:27; Philippians 4:8-9), and we don't have to be afraid (Psalm 145:18-19).

When I prayed for His vision, I saw a secure, smart woman who used the former pain of disordered eating to comfort men and women around me. On a larger scale, I envisioned developing a class and writing a book to encompass the elements of freedom and truth.

The vision didn't happen overnight. There were years of learning and living to do, but the choice to move toward the vision was immediate. Your vision doesn't have to include a ministry or a guest appearance on *Oprah* to be a powerful vision. My prayer for you, my pleading with God, is that you'll see yourself free from food's control. Let this be the day that you, the underdog, triumph over disordered eating, the bully. Redefine yourself as a *free* person regarding food, and seize the gift God gives you as a recreated person.

I once heard Larry Crabb use the illustration of a banquet table in a talk he gave for professional baseball wives. He explained that we're invited to a banquet hosted by our King (Christ). Because we're heirs of the King, it's our rightful place to sit at the table with Him and enjoy the feast. But instead, we crawl on the floor under the table with the dogs, looking for nasty crumbs to devour instead of the feast itself.[3]

So it is for those who choose to stay stuck in the past. The crumbs of past wounds and hurts become a measly diet rather than the rich provisions of the King. The ability to redefine and recreate who we are is one of the greatest blessings God bestows on humanity. Your story is never over unless you choose for it to be over. A wild adventure with God awaits.

SEAL YOUR HEALING

It's important to *seal* your healing experience regarding food and to mark it as a monument where you've had a personal encounter with God. Throughout the Bible, when someone had an experience or revelation from God, the person often built a stone monument or renamed the place where this mighty encounter took place. When Abraham received word from God that his descendants would inherit an expansive land, he stopped and built an altar there. Between chapters twelve and fourteen in the Book of Genesis are four monuments mentioned that were built by Abraham to mark his encounters with God. Moses and Joshua followed this same pattern of monument-marking.

Do you believe God wants to have an encounter with you? He loves to stir the hearts of His people, and He loves it when we mark it as a treasured moment in our lives.

I have small stones everywhere in my house. Some are on my desk and kitchen ledge to remind me of an encounter I've had with God. There's a stone that represents Truly Fed and the healing I've had with food, a stone that marks healing in my marriage, and one that represents restoration in the life of one of my daughters. There's nothing holy or magical about these stones—they just serve as reminders that God is the healer, protector, and lover of my soul. By marking my encounters with God as monuments, it draws me to remembrance and fuels my certainty that I'll never return to my old behavior.

A scripture in Proverbs has always made me feel a bit sick to my stomach. It says, "Like a dog that returns to its vomit is a fool who repeats his folly" (Proverbs 26:11).

Have you ever seen a dog return to its vomit? Disgusting! But that's often how we live. After feeling God's touch and experiencing wisdom and healing in our lives, why would we want to return to our vomit? It's foolishness and folly, yet at times that's exactly how we end up.

In *The Diet Alternative* Diane Hampton talks about the connection to leaving our house empty (Matthew 12:43) after we've experienced some degree of healing. She paraphrases it by writing,

> Jesus tells us that when the unclean spirit is gone out of a man (the spirit of overeating) that it looks for another place to live. But if it can't find one, it returns. If the house is empty (still watching TV), it brings seven other spirits more wicked than itself (binge, condemnation, depression). You cannot stand on God's Word without a foundation. Don't leave your house empty—fill yourself with God's Word. You can't stand on His Word if you don't know His Word. Find scriptures to help you to not worry or feel negative emotions.[4]

We can seal healing with the knowledge of God's truth about us found in His Word and by marking our healing in an almost ceremonious fashion.

We live in a middle-class neighborhood of manicured lawns and predictable pedigree of house grooming. I sometimes giggle to myself as I think of the monuments I would like to build to my Lord in thanks for His grace and deliverance in my life. I would have huge stone monuments dotting my front and back yards. They might look like a bad rendition of today's classy barbeque pits, but I would build them. At the top of each stone monument I would place large crosses to show my remembrance of Jesus' sacrifice. Can you imagine my homeowners association's attitude toward this? It's a good thing I choose smooth stones I buy in bulk at Hobby Lobby. Sometimes I write dates and names on them. As I sit here writing today, I'm looking at one that says "Truly Fed, September 2007." That's when I started my proposal for this book. It was a sacred moment I wanted to keep as a monument with God.

As you go through your days, when you experience a time that you know God has encountered you, mark it with something visual you can use to remember it—a stone, seashell, or small trinket. A week of binge-free eating, a sense of new peace and joy with food, a release of stringent food restrictions, waking up in the morning thinking about something other than what you'll eat that day—all merit a monument marker. Get your stones out. Seal your healing with the tender remembrance of the power of God's encounters with you.

GERI'S STORY

One night a beautiful woman with caramel-colored skin and soft eyes asked if she could speak with me. She shared a stunning story.

She had attended one of my classes on breaking generational cycles and was deeply moved. On her way home from work the next night, she thought about what she wanted to eat for dinner. She had been following the principle of sowing seeds to God with her eating and had been eating a morning meal, then sowing seeds until dinner. A hamburger is what she wanted, so she fixed one and sat down to enjoy it. As she was cooking, she turned on the television set to a Lifetime movie. It was a movie she had seen several times before. In the movie a woman was raped. As Geri lifted the burger to her mouth, she heard the Lord speak to her heart, *This is why you eat!*

She put the burger down and pushed away from the table. She pulled out her journal and began to write her painful story from beginning to end. It's a story she had never told. "As I wrote, I felt the Lord stroking me," Geri remembers. "It's as though He whispered to me how sorry He was that I went through this."

Geri was raped when she was 19 years old by a man who climbed through her bedroom window. After the tragic incident, she felt isolated and alone. She didn't feel as though she could tell her family what had happened. She was raised to be perfect, and anything less than perfect wasn't accepted in her family. Rape was too great a stain for her perfectionist parents to allow, so she kept it to herself.

One of her friends was moving from Colorado to California, so she decided to move with her. She knew she was running away, but she didn't care. It was a passage of escape she welcomed.

Geri lived in San Diego for three years, and her life deteriorated into the horror of alcohol, drugs, and promiscuity. She figures that she slept with more than forty men during that span of time.

She tried to stop her devastating habits, but sheer willpower wasn't enough to lead her away from the people and the lifestyle. She sang in a band, and she recalls how fans walked by and put drugs into her hand. The cycle of destruction was so deep that she was drowning in her own behavior.

After three years, she moved to San Francisco and changed jobs. But soon she became involved with a married man, and her self-esteem plummeted to a new low. She decided to move back to Denver, and during that time she rededicated her life to Christ.

Although her life was on a new path, she still had holes and voids in her heart. Leaving behind the old vices that typically aren't accepted in Christian circles—drugs, alcohol, sex—she turned to an acceptable vice: food. Her small frame ballooned as she tried to eat away her sorrow.

On her way home from a meeting, she started down the highway contemplating the notion of breaking cycles and generational pain. Suddenly her mouth dropped open, and she was so overcome with emotion that she had to pull over to the side of the road.

"It was as though my life flashed before me. The Lord showed me that right after I was saved many years ago, I had an affair with a married man. I went on to have several affairs, and each relationship flashed before me. I saw the rape and all the mind-bending choices I made after it. I asked for forgiveness and the courage to be free from my past."

Bawling like a baby on the side of the highway, Geri opened the door to freedom that night. She doesn't use food as her excuse anymore. If she eats too much, she now simply cuts back. Her weight is stable, and her freedom is glorious. Geri later received counseling to further her freedom. When we recently got together for lunch, she softly commented, "The idea of freedom can be terrifying, because you really have to look at who you are."

Sitting across the table from this strong woman, I thought how grateful I am for her story. Her chains are gone, and a sweet spirit oozes from her presence. Only our great God can heal so completely and replace the burdensome chains with ribbons of delight.

TAKING OFF THE CHAINS OF THE PAST

When I teach Truly Fed classes, the week we deal with the past and generational cycles is typically the most profound. Last summer, as I prepared to teach that lesson, I went to Home Depot and bought the heaviest metal chain I could find. As I stood before the class, I draped the chain around my shoulders. It was painfully uncomfortable, and it clanked every time I moved. I taught the entire class with this heavy chain around my shoulders. There was no way anyone was going to forget it was there. At the end of class, I draped the chain over a cross that I had stood on a table behind me. We gathered around that cross and prayed, asking God to help us place our chains on the cross.

What are your burdensome chains? What cycles of behavior are you ready to have lifted from your shoulders?

Chains don't just get up and move on their own. They need your permission. Once you grant that permission, the clanking and heaviness no longer bind you.

Personal Morsels

Our past is part of what makes us who we are, but it's not the complete story. Thankfully, we can count on God to heal us from the past and renew the future. Read Isaiah 42:6-9, and mark it in your Bible. This scripture boldly states God's intention to recreate a future that crushes the darkness of the past. Let's look at the first part of this scripture:

> I am the LORD, I have called you in righteousness, I will also hold you by the hand and watch over you, and I will appoint you as a covenant to the people, as a light to the nations, to open blind eyes, to bring out prisoners from the dungeon, and those who dwell in darkness from the prison.

How have your eyes been blind regarding your behavior with food?

_____

_____

_____

_____

_____

_____

_____

_____

_____

How have you dwelled in darkness in the prison of disordered eating—dieting, purging, severe food restriction, self-image?

_____

_____

_____

_____

_____

_____

_____

_____

_____

_____

Verse 9 of this passage states, "Behold, the former things have come to pass, Now I declare new things; before they spring forth I proclaim them to you."

You've acknowledged the "former things" that have kept you dwelling in the darkness of past habits and behaviors. What are the "new things" you desire in your relationship with food?

_____

_____

_____

_____

_____

_____

_____

_____

_____

God says that He declares new things with you! The desires you have for freedom and hope with food are the desires He has for you. God says that before they spring forth, He proclaims them to you. Grasp the fact that not only is God declaring and shouting new things about you regarding food—He is also proclaiming them!

Take a moment to mark this time as a personal monument with God. If you're skeptical or just not feeling it, do it anyway. God says, "Before they spring forth, I proclaim it to you."

It's tempting to think, *When I lose weight, then I'll mark a monument,* or *When I'm not so consumed by food . . .* or *When I see a major change in my behavior . . .* or *When I stop purging. . . .* God says *before* they spring forth. If He's already proclaiming your freedom, shouldn't you believe it?

I know you're tired and you're sick of empty promises. But if you can muster up even an ounce of faith to mark this time as a monument in your life with God, I believe you'll be blessed.

When I doubt, when I face the overwhelming heartache of empty belief, I speak this scripture: "May the God of hope fill [me] with all joy and peace in believing, that [I] may abound in hope by the power of the Holy Spirit" (Romans 15:13).

Believe, dear friends, for a healed past. Believe for a new future. Believe for a life free from prison's darkness. Oswald Chambers says, "Yielding to Jesus will break every form of slavery in any human life."[5]

That's a promise you can take to the bank!

SIX

Whose Voice Is That?

Sometimes they come in the night—voices. The voices feed us a steady diet of lies and half-truths that are just strong enough to gain a foothold in our minds, robbing us of sleep, causing us to wring our hands in worry. It's as though a tape recorder, stuck on the "play" button, is repeatedly assaulting us with a stream of lies.

Actually, this is exactly what *is* happening as we endure an onslaught from Satan, whom Jesus himself referred to as "the father of lies." Although Satan's lies are destructive to those in their path, because there is no truth in lies, they're just smoke and mirrors in his limited assault arsenal against God's children.

In the Book of Revelation there is a profound scripture that describes this predicament. It says, "Now the salvation, and the power, and the kingdom of our God and the authority of His Christ have come, for the accuser of our brethren has been thrown down, who accuses them before our God day and night" (Revelation 12:10).

When it comes to food, have you ever felt as if you're accused by voices day and night?

If we gathered together one hundred struggling eaters and asked them what the voices they hear in their heads say on a regular basis, their answers would probably sound something like this:

- I'll never be able to have a nice figure, so why try?
- I can't eat like a normal person.
- If I let go of my hold over food, I'll spiral out of control.
- I'm disgusted with my stomach, hips—my shape as a whole. I look hideous.
- This is the cross I have to bear in this life.

- I can't share my innermost secrets about food with others, because they'll think I'm crazy.
- I have no self-discipline. I'm a selfish failure.

Sound familiar? The voices are relentless and cruel. Sometimes we're so accustomed to listening to them that we forget they're foreign. They're enemy invaders in our minds. Yet we tolerate them and at times even welcome the familiarity of their presence.

A beautiful, slender young woman named Deb shared her struggle: "I wish I could just push an 'off' button to the voices in my head. I'm constantly listening to the whisper that I'll never be thin enough, and my mind will never be free from pain with food."

Her thoughts echo in our own hearts as well. Much of our struggles with food are battles played out in our minds. Max Lucado calls this mind game "DTP": Destructive Thought Patterns.[1]

DTPs are patterns of thought that destroy the truth *in* our lives, God's purpose *for* our lives, and the confidence that He will lead us away from destruction into a new way of living. DTPs have the power to crush anything in their path. Just ask anyone who has dieted for decades, throws up ritually, exercises incessantly, or starves himself or herself daily. The voices are so loud and accepted in our minds that the truth can barely trickle into the infected regions.

God has His own name for these voices. In Isaiah He calls them "destroyers and devastators." He boldly tells us that these foreign invaders don't belong, and He promises that they will depart from us.

"Behold, I have inscribed you on the palms of My hands; your walls [your thoughts, inner voices] are continually before Me. Your builders hurry [new thoughts of freedom and seed-sowing]; your destroyers and devastators will depart from you" (Isaiah 49:16-17).

WHAT ARE DESTROYERS AND DEVASTATORS?

Destroyers and devastators walk hand-in-hand with one another. To *destroy* is to dismantle what was once working or functional. To *devastate* is to demolish, leaving a trail of fear, heartache, abuse, and pain. It's important to remember that Satan's primary weapons against us—lies—all have the same goal: to destroy and devastate.

In his book *When the Enemy Strikes*, Charles Stanley writes,

Never forget the devil's purposes:
- To draw you away from God
- To thwart God's purpose for your life
- To deny the glory of God in your life
- To destroy you in any way he can, including physical health.[2]

The misuse of food is a tool that Satan uses to draw us away from God. As a matter of fact, as long as we're preoccupied with a poor self-image, bizarre eating patterns, and obsession with dieting or purging, we're limited in the freedom and joy we can live out with God. It's not that they can't coexist— it's just that they aren't firing on all cylinders.

God has a lot to say about freedom. His words bring hope, as Paul explains:

It was for freedom that Christ set us free; therefore keep standing firm and do not be subject again to a yoke of slavery (*Galatians 5:1*).

There is therefore now no condemnation for those who are in Christ Jesus. For the law of the Spirit of life in

Christ Jesus has set you free from the law of sin and death (*Romans 8:1-2*).

That, in reference to your former manner of life, you lay aside the old self, which is being corrupted in accordance with the lusts of deceit, and that you be renewed in the spirit of your mind, and put on the new self, which in the likeness of God has been created in righteousness and holiness of the truth (*Ephesians 4:22-24*).

Any voice that opposes God's call to freedom in a believer's life is false. Any voice that stifles hope or mocks the belief that we can live free from bondage is not from God. He is our greatest cheerleader, and He is the provider of our finest victories.

WHERE DO THESE VOICES COME FROM?

Not every voice in our heads is from Satan. Once he has effectively invaded the mental image we have of ourselves, we do a fine job on our own of hitting the replay button on the negative voices. After we hear these damaging statements many times a day, the statements begin to seem like truth, and the pain they cause becomes more powerful.

In addition to the lies Satan tells us, we typically hear voices from three other sources:

1. Our parents (spoken and unspoken)
2. Friends, teachers, or casual acquaintances
3. Our culture

The parents' role is critical in the healthy development of a child. When parents use their words to encourage children and teach them inner discipline and strength, peace and confidence are usually the result. On the other hand, if parents lash out at their children with their words, tearing them down or snubbing them with disinterest, a void is left in the children that seeks to be filled.

I remember a playmate I had as a child who went through a season of her life spilling milk and dropping things. Her mom used to say, "You're so clumsy!" Soon, every time my friend got near her mom, she dropped or spilled something. The voice reminding her of her clumsiness was constantly in her mind, making it easy to fulfill what the voice told her she was—clumsy.

The voices of friends, casual acquaintances, and teachers can also play in our heads. Mindless comments such as "You look bigger—have you gained weight?" can devastate us, even if the comments were made innocently.

I realized early in my career as a teacher that I had a unique gift entrusted to me in the time I had with my students. I could *believe* them to be the kind of students I hoped they would be—or merely tolerate them to get through the year. I saw this play out clearly in a young man named Daylon. He came to me as an angry, smart, bullying third-grader. I poured my heart out to him in the form of discipline plans, encouragement, love, and honesty. He about sucked the life out of me, but I began to see small slivers of progress. By the end of the year, at an all-school assembly where Daylon was receiving a citizenship award, his comments were "I've never received an award before. Mrs. Meacham taught me how to change my life."

To this day I could tear up as I think of how easy it would have been to give up on Daylon. Thanks to the encouragement of his second-grade teacher and the words of hope I showered over him, Daylon became a great student and friend.

Even small and seemingly inconsequential voices add up in the recesses of our minds. They spill over into our actions and beliefs.

The voice of our culture is another steady influence that molds our minds. Thin, perfect bodies grace the covers of magazines; air-brushed perfection is dangled before us as the epitome of beauty. The voice of our culture is always changing and relentlessly pushing us toward conforming to the latest new trend.

One thing is for sure: it's futile to devote our lives to pursuing and complying with these standards. Only God's voice offers freedom, hope, and vitality. Recognizing where our inner voices come from is the first step in breaking the unhealthy hold they have on us.

WHAT THESE VOICES TELL US ABOUT FOOD

I believe inner voices have three main messages they repeat to us that focus on our relationships with food and lead us into unhealthy responses:

The frustrated dieter voice

The anorexic voice

The bulimic/purger voice

1. The frustrated dieter voice: Those of us who have dieted relentlessly are accustomed to a sorority of voices in our minds. Although the voices may vary slightly, they typically have the same chants and rings to them.

The first voice a dieter hears is that of determination: "You can do it!" "Get the right program or diet or plan, and you'll lose this weight for good!" This is the voice encouraging us back on the diet merry-go-round, even though we've been on that ride before and know it only takes us in circles! Around and around we go—counting calories, carbs, portions; restricting intake; and begging the pounds to fall off our bodies.

Soon the voices that originally cheered us on seem to change their allegiance and their message.

"Go ahead and cheat—you deserve it!"

"You're just going to gain back the weight you've lost anyway, so why not indulge?"

"See? I knew you couldn't do it!"

I call this the cycle of determination/frustration. The voices badger and beat us so effectively that we stay bound to their control like a battered child.

After this cycle plays out, new voices emerge. These voices say things like—

"I'll never be happy with my body. Its lumps, bumps, and humps are here forever."

"I'm just not disciplined enough. I have no self-control."

These are the voices that trap us into a state of mind that tells us that no matter what we do, this is the way we are, so we had better deal with it. The problem is that this *isn't* the way we are. It's not even close! God created us to be free and confident, healthy and whole—not disgusted and defeated. These "resolution" voices then lead to "acceptance" voices: "I love food too much to change. Food is my only joy and comfort."

This is when we give up the fight for a while. But after languishing in the land of overeating for a period, we jump back in line at the merry-go-round, and here we go again.

2. **The anorexic voice:** I'm often asked what the signs of anorexia are. For sake of clarity, I would like to share what Wendy Oliver Pratt, M.D., considers anorexic behavior:

- Failure to maintain a minimum body weight
- An intense fear of becoming fat, despite being underweight

- A distorted body image and the belief that one is over-weight
- Basing self-esteem on weight or body shape
- Denial of the seriousness of being underweight
- If female, missing at least three consecutive periods (or has periods only when taking hormones)[3]

With this criteria in place, it's easy to see why anorexic voices are often the trickiest to battle. More than any other types of voices, these are laced with distortion. A person listening to these voices may have started out believing statements that do have some truth to them. For instance, it's true that fruits, vegetables, and protein are good for you. It's a distortion to believe that if you ingest bread, pasta, sweets, or pizza, you'll instantly gain weight or feel sick.

It's true that exercise is good for you, but it's a distortion to believe that you must exercise every day to maintain a healthful weight. These voices run on an ounce of truth and a gallon of lies. Most anorexics agree that there are similar voices that veil their thinking:

"I'm not thin enough. There's still room to be thinner."

"I can't ever eat normally; I'll risk gaining weight."

"I'm in total control of my body and my life."

"What's thin for someone else is too fat for me."

Someone struggling with anorexia may read these lies and think there's absolutely nothing wrong with any of these voices. But I know many women who struggle with these lies—I've believed them myself—and there's a lot wrong with them.

I know women who have lost all hope of having children because their reproductive system has been damaged due to starvation. Dental and skin problems are common in these women, but there's an isolated, rebellious spirit that vehemently defends their behavior. It's as though a skilled kidnapper has brainwashed them into believing that this is a better way to live.

One day I planned to meet a friend who struggled with anorexia for coffee and a visit. At the last minute I had to change the location of our meeting due to car problems I was having. She panicked as she shared with me that she had already added the calories in the coffee she would order to what she would allow herself to ingest that day, and she didn't feel as if she could change our plans. Rational thinking escapes the anorexic as the lying voices continue to drive strange behavior.

Many of the voices that speak to an anorexic perpetuate fear. Some women have an overweight mother, so they vow never to look like her regardless of the price. The fear of looking like Mom fuels a starvation mentality.

For others, it's perfectionism. Some of us believe that anything less than perfect is failure: perfect daughter, perfect mother, perfect wife, perfect friend, perfect employee. It's unachievable, of course. We were never meant to be perfect in those areas; we use food as a means of control when our circumstances can't be manipulated.

Most of the women I know who struggle with anorexia have similar personalities: sweet, kind-hearted, generous, yet wildly rebellious when it comes to food. In the mind of an anorexic, starving herself is a way to make a statement about her life without breaking the "I'm a nice person" code of behavior she's bound to.

3. The bulimic/purger voice: The person who follows the bulimic/purger voice eats in binges; during these episodes, the bulimic consumes much more food than is normal and feels that his or her eating is out of control:

- Repeatedly uses laxatives, fasting, vomiting, excessive exercise, diuretics, or other drugs in order to lose weight
- Experiences binge eating and purging at least twice a week
- Bases his or her self-esteem primarily on weight and body shape
- Is not anorexic. Most bulimics maintain an average weight.[4]

Bulimic voices encourage the hearer toward secrecy. The voices taunt the believer to submerge into a dark world of hushed secrets where their actions will remain unnoticed or untouched by those around them. The messages are things like—

"Eat all you want now, and get rid of it later in private."

"Pills, laxatives, and excessive exercise are the perfect remedy for binge eating."

"Throwing up is easy. What goes down can simply come back up."

After initial success at ridding the body of its excess intake, this plan often backfires, and the binges often put weight on the bulimic.

A friend of mine shared with me that she had perfected the art of throwing up so successfully that she could vomit without making a sound. It didn't matter if she was at a dinner party, her parent's home, or a crowded bathroom at work. This talent was her pride and joy, and her inner voices applauded her behavior. But when she began to quit losing weight and actually gained a few pounds while practicing these rituals, she pressed on to even more extreme behavior to try to get a handle on the weight. The voices that initially promised weight loss and control by eliminating what's eaten eventually turned on the believer, leaving her with a chaotic habit that no longer worked.

WINNING THE BATTLE FOR OUR MINDS

When I was on the verge of suicide due to my struggle with anorexia and compulsive overeating, I remember calling a friend and saying, "I feel as if there's a war going on in my head!" I cried in a state of near-panic, "It's as though there are knives slicing their way through my brain!"

She calmly said, "There *is* a war playing out in your mind, Gari. You're leaving the turf of confusion, sin, and defeat and moving toward the truth of Christ."

Years earlier, her words would have seemed crazy to me, but now they made perfect sense. It was a relief to know I wasn't losing my mind. I was actually gaining a new mind.

Paul describes this battle perfectly:

> Though we walk in the flesh, we do not war according to the flesh, for the weapons of our warfare are not of the flesh, but divinely powerful for the destruction of fortresses. We are destroying speculations and every lofty thing raised up against the knowledge of God, and we are taking every thought captive to the obedience of Christ (*2 Corinthians 10:3-5*).

Paul uses war terms to emphasize the seriousness of this battle, words like *battle, weapons, power, destruction, fortresses;* we aren't talking about gardening here—this is a war for our minds.

It's wise to ask yourself, *What are the "voice fortresses" that are at the core to my actions? What are the speculations and lofty things that are raised up against God in my mind?*

It may simply be a paralyzed way of living with food. In a manner of speaking, we tie God's hands so that they're powerless to defeat the voices we listen to. Fortresses aren't built overnight. They've been built, brick by brick, over a span of time. The voices we listen to are part of these fortresses and must be considered.

One of the greatest examples of defeating negative voices can be found in the story of David and Goliath. Nothing about this story is easy. We can't romanticize it or lessen the degree of internal struggle that must have taken place in David's heart, mind, and trembling muscles.

David was a young shepherd who divided his time between tending to Saul—playing a harp to calm his nerves—and tending sheep. He wasn't even invited to the battle when Saul took his army out to meet the Philistines. But God had a plan, and He sent David to meet his brothers at the battle site with food and greetings from their father.

Prior to David's arrival, the Israelite camp looked a lot like a little league team facing the New York Yankees. A man standing almost nine feet tall, with muscles and mouth to match, taunted the army of God for forty days, morning and night. He was a cocky Philistine named Goliath, who based his high opinion of himself solely on his looks, physical strength, and reputation.

As David was talking to his brothers, Goliath came out and began his daily tease. The Israelite army ran away in fright. "'Have you seen the giant?' the men asked" (1 Samuel 17:24, NLT).

The voices David heard from these running soldiers were the voices of fear, terror, and defeated resignation. These voices begged him to join in their ranks of hopeless hand-wringing.

David probed for more information as he ignored the initial voices he heard from those around him. He asked what a man might receive for killing this Philistine who so flagrantly defied the army of the living God. As they filled him in on the reward, a new set of voices chimed in. These voices were even more deadly than those of the fleeing soldiers, because they came from his own brother Eliab.

"'What are you doing around here anyway?' he demanded. 'What about those few sheep you're supposed to be taking care of? I know of your pride and deceit. You just want to see the battle'" (1 Samuel 17:28, NLT).

Ouch! The sting of these sarcastic voices cut to the heart of who David was.

- "Why are you here?" (You're not welcome. You aren't good enough to be a part of this.)
- "Shouldn't you be with those few sheep you're in charge of?" (You aren't worthy. You're a small-time loser who will never amount to anything.)
- "I know what you're really like—filled with pride and deceit." (I know the real you. You're despicable and filled with undesirable traits.)

If ever voices could stop someone in their tracks, you would think these could. Yet David presses on. He replies to his brother, "What have I done now? I'm just asking a question."

And here's where David becomes a hero, even before he defeats Goliath. David chooses to ignore, and even fight against, the voices crowding his head. He walks away from his brother's damaging voice, the voice of fear from his peers, and listens to God's voice.

Even Saul had a voice when David offered to fight the Philistine. "Don't be ridiculous!" he said. "You're just a boy!"

Instead of sinking into submission, David remembered what God had done in his life. He recalled how as a shepherd he had fought off lions and bears with his bare hands to protect his sheep.

He was ready. He was prepared. God had used an unlikely training ground to mold him into a capable warrior. He just had to listen to the right voices.

Even as he faced Goliath, I believe David may have been shaking, but he allowed God's voice of strength, assurance, and freedom to capture his courage.

What is your Goliath? And what voices spew from this giant's mouth toward you? Our Goliaths taunt and tease, but with God's voice captivating our minds, we can overcome them as David did.

HOW DO WE TAKE THOUGHTS CAPTIVE?

Taking our thoughts captive to the obedience of Christ is a deliberate action. It's not passive—it's aggressive, and we must be aggressive in our fight against negative voices.

I would like to offer a few strategies that are both visual and tactile in their approaches to quieting these choruses. Psalm 56 paints a beautiful picture of how God views the pain in our lives.

> You keep track of all my sorrows. You have collected all my tears in your bottle. You have recorded each one in your book. My enemies will retreat when I call to you for help. This I know: God is on my side! *(Psalm 56:8-9, NLT).*

Can you imagine the bottle God collects our tears in? I picture a beautifully colored glass, etched with roses or floral design. A glass cork fits snugly into the top of the bottle so no tear can spill out or be wasted. I suggest you go by a craft store and purchase a bottle or glass jar that you love. Set it on your kitchen counter or another prominent place in your home, and write out the negative things the voices in your head say to you. Each slip of paper represents a voice from the past or present that impacts your thinking in a negative way. Continue to place these voices into the jar, realizing that God seals those tears in *His* bottle. Your enemies—hurtful voices, destructive behaviors—will retreat when you call to God for help. Go on the offensive instead of simply reacting in frustration. God is on your side!

Earlier I mentioned a phrase I say to myself: "I don't do that anymore!" Many women feel this is helpful to repeat when sowing seed to God regarding food. This phrase can also be changed to "I don't believe that anymore" when fighting off negative voices.

One woman shared with me how she put her negative voices to rest. She took her small children to the movies, and as she left the restroom she caught a glimpse of herself in the mirror. "You're fat and unattractive!" the voice screamed at her. There was a time she would have sunk down and allowed the voices to continue to prod her, ruining her time with her children. Instead, she talked back to the voice: "I don't believe that anymore. God says I'm free and whole in Him. I don't have to listen to this voice anymore. And I won't!" She promptly walked out of the restroom and had a lovely day with her kids.

Another way to battle negative voices is to put them through what I call the "voice filter." If any voice you hear doesn't have one of the following characteristics attached to it, throw it out! It doesn't line up with God's voice over your life.

- Peace (Philippians 4:7)
- Freedom (John 8:31-32)
- Hope (Romans 15:13)
- Purpose (Philippians 2:13)

The character of God is defined by peace, freedom, hope, and purpose. Like a strainer that lets the cooking water drip off perfect pasta, so the voices that cloud our minds must drip off our self-image and hope.

CHOOSING TO BELIEVE WHAT IS TRUE

What we choose to believe about ourselves greatly impacts how we live our lives. God promises to give us new life when we walk away from the old. But in order to walk away from the old, we have to be convinced that the new life we're walking toward is God-ordained and worthy.

Old Life

This is a people plundered and despoiled; All of them are trapped in caves [kitchens], or hidden away in prisons [behind closed doors, over toilets, or cloaked in secrecy]; They have become a prey with none to deliver them, And a spoil, with none to say, "Give them back!" (Isaiah 42:22).

New Life

Behold, the former things have come to pass, Now I declare new things; Before they spring forth I proclaim them to you (Isaiah 42:9).

God proclaims new things over our lives: freedom, truth, vitality, victory, endurance, and assurance. We simply have to agree with Him.

The fortresses and voices that have controlled us for so long finally have a foe. Their negative roars and incessant sniping must stop when faced with the peaceful strength of Christ's truth. God utters His shout and war cry over us. Together we will prevail against His enemies.

Personal Morsels

According to author Tim Hansel, studies have shown that when we talk at a normal rate, we speak about one hundred twenty words a minute. But psychologists tell us that when we self-talk—that is, carry on a conversation with ourselves inside our heads—we speak at a rate of about *thirteen hundred* words a minute.[5]

It gives me a headache to even consider this amount of chatter in my head! Hansel also points out that the bad news is that seventy percent of our self-talk is negative!

Look up 2 Corinthians 10:5, and write it below:

_____

_____

_____

_____

_____

It's interesting that the scripture starts by instructing us to take thoughts captive. Joanna Weaver adds to this verse by saying, "However, it isn't enough to take the thoughts captive. According to 2 Corinthians 10:5, I must also bring them into obedience to Christ. That means that after exposing the lies with truth, I need to promptly hand them over to Jesus."[6]

Write out your most glaring negative thoughts. Can you think of where or when they began to surface?

_____

_____

_____

_____

_____

How can you hand these thoughts over to Jesus in a tangible way?

_____

_____

_____

_____

_____

What are the "Goliaths" you're facing right now? What voices are you hearing concerning them?

_____

_____

_____

_____

_____

Read Luke 22:39-46. What kind of voices do you think Jesus heard that night, and how did He reckon with them?

_____

_____

_____

_____

_____

SEVEN

The Pleasing Texture of Freedom and Success

He Was Only a Chocolate Chip Cookie

He was only a chocolate chip cookie, but I loved him. I met him at a party. There he was at the end of the buffet—a loner, the last one on the plate. He had a certain something—a sweetness, a sensuality. He was one hot cookie.

I felt as if I'd always known him, always hungered for him. When he looked at me with those warm brown eyes, I melted. Before I knew it, I had my hands on him. After that night we were inseparable. With him, I could be myself. He didn't seem to care what mood I was in, how I looked, even if I gained weight. Together we had the recipe for happiness. No one satisfied me like Chip.

Then things changed. My friends said he was no good for me. He started giving me heartburn. I felt crummy. It had to end.

Now we've gone our separate ways. I hardly think of him anymore. Oh, if I see a certain TV commercial, a particular magazine ad, a coupon for 10 cents off—that old longing returns. And when we run into each other at the supermarket, we nod; we're friendly, but it's over.[1]

Long ago someone handed me this story on a greeting card. I chuckled as I read it and thought of my own chocolate chip cookie stories. I realized that even a hottie like Mr. Chip can't seduce me into returning to my old ways. It's over. We're done. I'm now seeing other important relationships in my life— and their names are *freedom, obedience,* and *hope.*

This chapter is mainly for readers who are struggling to lose weight. It's by far the most difficult chapter for me to write.

The words *freedom* and *obedience* seem to be at odds with one another at first glance. Does freedom just happen? Is it a miraculous occurrence from out of nowhere that knocks us over? Freedom does have a price, and that price is our obedience. When Jesus said, "You shall know the truth, and the truth shall set you free" (John 8:32, NKJV), He was insisting that we be in an active state of *knowing*. Knowing can be tough. It means letting go of excuses, strongholds, and lies in order to seek the greater good through obedience. Seeking out the truth won't benefit us in any way if we don't obediently follow the principles truth reveals to us.

One summer while I was teaching the Truly Fed course, we came to the lesson that focused on freedom and obedience. A pleasant woman who struggled with overeating raised her hand. "I thought this wasn't a diet, Gari," she said. I responded by assuring her that we weren't talking about a diet but rather the freedom that comes from a commitment to obedience and discipline.

She sat quietly through the remainder of the class, but after that, she never returned. From what I gathered, she thought Truly Fed would be a magic bullet for weight loss. She would eat all she wanted and be free! When concepts such as *obedience, self-control*, and *discipline* showed up, she checked out.

For most of us, years of failure and defeat have convinced us that we have no self-control. We don't believe we can be obedient to a smarter way of viewing food, because our past has been punctuated by poor choices. To understand our choices and behavior, we must fully grasp *why* we eat the way we do.

In her book *When Food Is Your Best Friend and Worst Enemy*, Jan Johnson notes that overeaters feel as if they're unworthy and that no one can love them just as they are. "It follows that if I believe I'm such a bad person, then I must hide my true self if anyone is going to like me. As we become more secretive about our compulsion, we feel we are so unlovable that we have to avoid intimacy, yet in public, we display a pseudo-confident image to get by.[2]

For those of us who are emotional eaters, food becomes the great ally. It becomes our closest confidant; it replaces others—and God.

Many persons believe that God doesn't care about their eating. They rationalize that He's far more concerned with the "biggies," such as infidelity, immorality, gossip, and lies. The truth is that God cares deeply about our eating. Anything that blocks our freedom and dependence on Him is a biggie in His eyes.

In many ways it's somewhat easy to shove our pain with food aside and convince ourselves that it's not all that bad. Because the act of eating is universal and something everyone needs to do every day, it's easy to hide compulsions in a blanket of complacency or denial. The truth is that compulsive overeaters are slaves to food.

Food beckons, and we follow.

Compulsion lies, and we listen.

Sadness seeps, and we cover.

I've often been approached by women who are confused as to whether or not they're compulsive overeaters. Some feel that they just love food but hate the results of overeating. Some insist that they don't eat too much; it just all goes to their hips! Others insist that slow metabolism is the culprit when they compare it to the metabolism of other women who don't seem to struggle with food.

Take a few moments to look at this quiz that Overeaters Anonymous uses to link behavior to compulsive eating.

You may be wondering what it means if a lot of your answers were affirmative. Typically, overeaters know their behavior is harmful but don't like the title "compulsive overeater."

Are You a Compulsive Eater?

1. Do you eat consistently when you're not hungry?
2. Do you go on eating binges for no apparent reason?
3. Do you have feelings of guilt and remorse after over-eating?
4. Do you give too much time and thought to food?
5. Do you look forward with pleasure and anticipation to the moments when you can eat alone?
6. Do you plan secret binges ahead of time?
7. Do you eat sensibly in front of others and make up for it when you're alone?
8. Is your weight affecting the way you live your life?
9. Do you resent others telling you to "use a little will-power" to stop overeating?
10. Despite evidence to the contrary, have you continued to assert that you can diet on your own whenever you wish?
11. Do you eat to escape from worries or troubles?
12. Have you ever been treated for obesity or a food-related condition?
13. Does your eating behavior make you or others un-happy?[3]

I'm convinced that most humans have at some time eaten to escape from worries or troubles or crave to eat at a time other than what's commonly designated for meals. This becomes compulsive behavior when it's habitual.

Jan Johnson notes, "Compulsions were thought to be behavioral only. Now we know that choices we make over and over about certain behaviors form a chemical path on the neurotransmitters in our brain. These paths make it likely that we'll repeat the behavior."[4]

BUFFET VERSUS BUFFET

In his first letter to the Corinthians, Paul is preaching a mighty sermon. He compares faith to running a race or competing in games. He writes, "Everyone who competes in the games exercises self-control in all things. . . . Therefore I run in such a way, as not without aim; I box in such a way, as not beating the air; but I *buffet* my body and make it my slave" (1 Corinthians 9:25, emphasis added).

The use of the word *buffet* intrigued me, so when I looked it up, I was surprised to see that it means "punch and beat." Is Paul talking about punching and beating his own body? In a spiritual sense, I guess so. He's talking about taking charge of his body, exercising self-control so his body is his slave and not the other way around. How often as compulsive overeaters we're the slaves to our bodies!

I find it humorous that the verb *buffet* is spelled exactly the same as the noun *buffet*—as in "all-you-can-eat" buffet.

For many of us, the all-you-can-eat buffet is a better description of our lives and patterns. Think back to the last time you visited a buffet. Chances are that you saw people with their plates heaped high with foods from every category: fried, roasted, baked, and poached. The well-worn carpet is a testimony to the many trips patrons make to keep their plates and stomachs full—and this is before they spot the dessert bar!

My kids loved buffets until they became aware of a few realities. My older daughter spoke up once when we were talking about where we should go to eat. "Mommy, I always feel yucky after the buffet. Let's go somewhere else!" After a little discussion, we deduced that the *yucky* feeling came from the lack of self-control that leads to both physical and mental anguish.

Let's look at the differences between *buffeting* our bodies for God and living in the "buffet" mentality.

Buffet: punch, beat, exercise self-control

- The mind dictates the body's consumption of food rather than robotic compulsion.
- You choose strength over momentary pleasure of taste.
- You're confident that appropriate choices and actions lead to health and well-being.
- You understand that long-term self-control doesn't allow you to fall into the "diet/failure/binge" trap.

Buffet: extreme consumption

- You eat for the moment with no regard for how it may feel later.
- You hate the behavior but love the quick satisfaction of taste buds more.
- You understand the long-term behavior but choose to deny or ignore the ramifications.
- You believe that self-control is unattainable.

The good news is that God doesn't just throw up His hands in frustration and say, "Why can't you just lose weight? Get it together!" Instead, He provides a steady stream of instruction and hope through His Word.

Later in that same letter to the Corinthians, Paul assures us that "No temptation has overtaken you but such as is common to man; and God is faithful, who will not allow you to be tempted beyond what you are able, but with the temptation will provide a way of escape also, that you may be able to endure it" (1 Corinthians 10:13).

Sometimes I want to scream to God, "Do you get it? Do you know how hard it is to walk away from food that's so enticing? Do you know how hard it is not to binge on a lot of food and throw it up later?"

If God would answer me audibly, He would assure me, "Yes, I do know." The scripture says *no* temptation, and that includes pie, cake, cookies, candy, burgers, pizza, pasta, and chips.

So how does this tie in with my battle cry for freedom rather than dieting? Is it possible to lose weight without denying ourselves certain foods we love?

It *is* possible, and I've done it for more than twenty years now. The behavior pattern is actually quite simple:

- Sow seed to God in your daily eating. If there are trouble foods that you routinely binge on in your eating pattern, sow those to God until you sense that you've retrained that habit.

- Think about the word *escape* that Paul mentioned when talking about temptations. To *escape* means to "get away from." Rather than going head to head in conflict with food, plan an escape route. When you feel the urge to overeat or eat when you're not at all hungry, physically remove yourself from the food. Sometimes it feels as if a "trance-like" force comes over you, beckoning you to eat food you don't need. Literally leave the room and make yourself do something else. Walk outside, clean a bathroom, take a bath, pick up your Bible and journal, play with your kids, call a friend—anything to get away from the temptation to overeat.

- Stay connected spiritually to God and food. Keep a constant vigil over your thoughts and intentions with food rather than what you'll eat next and how many calories are in each bite. Put these scriptures, or any other scriptures you love, on the kitchen cabinets, refrigerator doors, countertops, and mirrors.

"Whether, then, you eat or drink or whatever you do, do all to the glory of God" (1 Corinthians 10:31).

"The kingdom of God is not eating and drinking, but righteousness and peace and joy in the Holy Spirit" (Romans 14:17).

"If you have died with Christ to the elementary principles of the world, why, as if you were living in the world, do you submit yourself to decrees such as, 'Do not handle, do not taste, do not touch!' These are matters which have, to be sure, the appearance of wisdom in self-made religion and self-abasement and severe treatment of the body, but are of no value against fleshly indulgence" (Colossians 2:20-21, 23).

SELF—CONTROL AND SIN BATTLES

Dieting and severely abasing our bodies, as the scripture in Colossians says, may look wise on the outside, but it doesn't get at the sin of gluttony. Only confession, prayer, and a resolve to live with new self-control based on seed-sowing and worship can get at those dark places.

In *Fingerprints of God*, singer and writer Jennifer Rothchild came to a dramatic conclusion. She realized that she struggled with overeating. As she listened to a tape on self-control, she noticed that she had consumed handfuls of dark chocolate, coffee with French vanilla cream, and a steady stream of jelly beans! By the end of the tape she was sickened by her behavior and realized that a person with no self-control is like a city with no walls. (Proverbs 25:28)[5]

In Old Testament times, cities were protected by the walls that were built around them. Watchmen looked over the walls day and night, alerting inhabitants of oncoming foreign invasion.

Compulsive overeaters have walls that are broken or have eroded over time. I often hear some who struggle with weight say, "But I don't eat that much!"

James O. Hill, director of the Center for Human Nutrition at the University of Colorado, states, "Scientists have searched for people who eat very little yet weigh a lot. What they have found instead are people who say they eat very little but turn out to eat quite a bit when their food intake is monitored. Rigorous studies show that it's impossible to be a really large person and not eat that much."[6]

The protective walls of self-control in our lives have to be maintained, and in some of our lives, rebuilt. (See Nehemiah 2:17.)

It's hard to imagine a battle against a chocolate chip cookie. Is eating a cookie and enjoying its smell, taste, and texture wrong? Of course not! Is eating a dozen cookies at one time wrong? You be the judge. Remember: gluttony is the problem, not a healthy desire to enjoy good food.

CHANGING MY RITUALS AND HABITS

My daughter calls me every morning on her way to work. She buzzes into the Starbucks near her office, Bible in hand, and enjoys coffee and conversation with God. This ritual is one she enjoys, and because she often works through lunch and is on a tight budget that includes Top Ramen Noodles and Lean Cuisine, she has dropped almost 40 pounds since graduating from college.

I asked her what she's doing differently. She sighed, sharing with me how she changed almost all of her poor habits. She hardly ever eats fast food, a former staple in her diet; she orders differently when at a restaurant; and she takes into account drinks and hidden eating times that she used to ignore. She eats everything she wants—but in moderation—and she's shifted her focus to be more "God" centered than "me" centered.

It's not easy to change some of our habits and rituals with food, but we have to ask ourselves, *What do I benefit from them?* Any unhealthy habit you nurture can be broken.

When a man approached Jesus, terrified for his son, who was having fits so desperate that he often fell into fire and water, he shouted that he had brought his son to Jesus' disciples and that they were useless. Jesus spoke healing over the boy, and he was well at once.

But the real teaching came when Jesus addressed His disciples. They asked Him why they hadn't been able to help the boy. Jesus said bluntly, "Because of the littleness of your faith." He then told them that if they had faith as tiny as a mustard seed, they could say to a mountain, "Move!" and it would have to. He finished His explanation by saying that this kind of situation needs prayer and fasting. (See Matthew 17:14-21.)

On my desk next to my computer I have a little bottle of mustard seeds that a dear friend gave me. They are the tiniest seeds you ever laid eyes on. I often pick up that bottle of seeds and reflect on the mountains I've told to move from my life: healing from an eating disorder, healing from a painful childhood, healing in a marriage that was broken, and healing in my children's lives. If God can move mountains with a small seed of faith, don't you think He can help you break the nagging habits regarding food that bind your body, mind, and spirit?

If you choose to "fast" a habit that's destructive, you move a mountain. If your habit is to consume food at night, fast this habit. If a particular food or event causes you problems—running through a drive-through or secretly consuming large amounts of certain types of food—fast these habits.

Remember: the goal is obedience through faith, not perfection. Whatever you've believed about your self-control and discipline in the past can be shed for new beliefs and habits.

THE PRAYER POSTURE

I often have conversations with my students about their body language. The ways they posture their bodies and eyes say a lot about what they convey to others and the state of their listening capacity. The same can be said for prayer. How we posture ourselves to interact with God is critical.

Are you constantly speaking, barking, demanding, crying, or whining to Him? Or do you have times of quiet reflection when you're postured to hear His still, small voice?

Are you turning your back to His presence and ignoring His words to you, even though you feel you're praying?

Do you roll your eyes when words of encouragement, hope, or change are shared with you? All these behaviors reflect your prayer posture, and our prayer posture is essential to experiencing God's healing with food.

In the book *In a Pit with a Lion on a Snowy Day*, Mark Batterson writes, "There are only two ways to live your life: survival mode or prayer mode. Survival mode is simply reacting to the circumstances around you. It's a pinball existence. And to be perfectly honest, it's predictable, monotonous, and boring. Prayer mode is the exact opposite. Your spiritual antenna is up and your radar is on. Prayer puts you in a proactive posture."[7]

Survival mode prayer sounds a little like Eeyore the donkey in Winnie the Pooh stories: grumpy, complaining, and gray. It's defeated and negative from the start. *It won't change anything, but I guess I'll pray about my eating problem* or *I'm so mad at you, God. Why didn't you make me another way?*

You can either live in a *survival/endure the heartache* mode or a *prayerful/change* mode. I remember when God showed me the difference.

My older daughter had entered college and was suffering a trauma that threatened her very existence. As she tried to deal with shattering memories and unwanted fear, she turned to alcohol and cutting to lessen the pain that was trapped inside her.

I thought I would lose my mind.

For the next few years, my prayers were offered from the rut I kept trying to climb out of. Every time I tried to pray for Brooke, I could see her only as she was—lonely, defeated, abusive, and injured. The dark clouds of winter didn't compare to the clouds in my heart. One day as I was praying from my rut, God sent a message to my heart: *Do you really believe I'm God? Do you believe I'm bigger than your heartache and fear?*

I stuttered a response back to Him, realizing that I wasn't believing much, just reacting from the uncomfortable perch in my rut. Over the course of the next few days, I felt God encouraging me to record the vision I had for my daughter (Habakkuk 2:2-3). I listed all the hopes I had for Brooke and her future. My list looked something like this:

- I see Brooke free from the bondage of alcohol and able to make choices centered around health and wholeness.
- I see Brooke having a blessed relationship with a husband who treasures her heart.
- I see Brooke ministering to women and girls who have suffered in similar ways—sharing the life of Jesus and His healing touch.
- I see Brooke living with passion for her God, knowing that He plucked her from the pit of despair and destruction.

I wish I could say that things changed overnight, but they didn't.

I did.

I picked several verses that I prayed faithfully around this vision every day. I'm not one who believes in formula prayer. You know—"Pray this way, and all your wishes will come true!" I just know that God was lifting me out of my rut praying and encouraging me toward vision praying.

Shortly after the time I began to change the way I prayed, I went to California to visit Brooke. She attended a sorority dance that night and came in at 4:00 A.M., drunk and depressed. Her date ignored her, and her friends were distant and unavailable. I rubbed her back as she threw up, and instead of sinking back into my former trench of defeated prayer, I silently recited my vision prayers over her.

By Brooke's senior year of college, we were seeing real progress. But what happened in the next three years was astonishing. She began to realize that drinking had a hold on her life and decided to let go of friends who continued to drag her down. She got a great job, worked hard, and began to feel a confidence and pride in work well done. She started to attend a wonderful church and began leading Bible studies for young girls. Her story was featured in a local magazine and impacted many with its honesty and hope.

I know that there's no such thing as a fairytale existence. Princesses get depressed and lonely, and princes are often not as charming as expected. But God is bigger than our ruts. I knew my prayer life would never be the same when I heard my daughter say, "Mom, you never saw me how I was. You always believed me to be something better!"

This is vision praying. We pray not from our ruts but from the hope of a vision for a better life.

A HOLY GROUND

One final thought regarding weight loss: your eating is your *holy ground* with the Lord. It's your treasured altar where you can offer sacrifices of either healing and discipline or out-of-control behavior.

After Moses heard God's words on the mountain called Horeb, he took off his shoes, because he knew he was on holy ground. (See Exodus 3.)

We spend most of our lives cursing our struggles with weight instead of recognizing that we're on holy ground with God. It's through this pain that we can see His ultimate glory. You alone are responsible for developing your personal history with God.

My prayer for you, beloved, is that your altars will be filled with the fruit of sacrifice, seeds for sowing, and restorative praise. God never turns away from an altar built to Him in humble adoration and belief. Posture yourself for victory and success. Pray with new vision and hope. God willingly accepts your offering.

Personal Morsels

Read and highlight Matthew 17:14-21. Then answer the following questions.

What does mustard seed faith look like regarding food? Example: *I will choose to break my habitual binge from seven o'clock to nine o'clock tonight.*

_____

_____

_____

_____

_____

_____

_____

_____

Has God ever moved a mountain in your life?

_____

_____

_____

_____

_____

_____

_____

_____

While thinking about the difference between the *buffet* versus *buffet* mentality, look up the following verses and answer the following questions.

1. **1 Timothy 4:6-8.** How does this verse apply to buffeting our bodies for God's purposes?

_____

_____

_____

_____

_____

_____

2. **Hebrews 12:11-13.** What is the reward of discipline? How does this apply to your struggle with food?

_____

_____

_____

_____

_____

_____

What is your prayer posture? Honestly evaluate how you communicate with God.

_____

_____

_____

_____

_____

_____

_____

Turn your response to the last question into a prayer. Share your hopes and desires with the Lord, and confess anything that gets in the way of a positive prayer posture.

_____

_____

_____

_____

_____

_____

_____

EIGHT

Sanity for the Long Haul

It's documented that up to ten million women and girls suffer from anorexia and bulimia, and an additional twenty-five million suffer from Eating Disorder Not Otherwise Specified (EDNOS).[1] These statistics are staggering, especially considering that they come only from within the United States.

What's happening to the minds and bodies of our women and girls? What kind of plague has descended upon us? It's as though our sanity monitor has checked out and left the building.

Let me assure you that your sanity is worth fighting for. As a matter of fact, it's a fight you must engage in. The other option is to live in silent resignation, believing that food will always be a blot on your mental health.

To begin this quest for sanity, we must name a formidable foe: *perfectionism*. When I first recognized that I had serious problems with food, the layers of frustration slowly became apparent. I was a perfectionist, and "all or nothing" was my mantra.

As a young girl, I was a motivator. I was the one everyone wanted on the kickball team at recess. Even though I wasn't the best athlete, I was the best encourager and led less-talented teams to victory because of my cheerleading.

As I grew older, I realized that there were many things in my life I couldn't control as easily as kickball players—the car accident that left my dad paralyzed, for instance. I could not control my mom's alcoholism and my struggle to be smarter, prettier, or more loveable.

Food was different, though. I teetered on the see-saw of overeating and feeling out of control to starving and feeling in control. I based my self-worth on how well I managed food. Perfectionism took over as my behavior with food defined my moods, opinions, and body image.

Grace Gusmano, a marriage and family therapist and eating disorder counselor, reflects, "In my work with women, I see them drift from a sense of wonder at their uniqueness. They give away their personal womanly power to a relationship and/or culture that enslaves them and prods them to reach the ideal size, weight, or career position. In the end they are profoundly dissatisfied because they can't reach perfection."[2]

Perfection in a fallen world is an illusion. We will never be perfect in our behavior with food, and we aren't meant to be. Sometimes we crave certain foods that our bodies need, sometimes we enjoy the variety and beauty of food that's not on a regimented food plan, and sometimes we eat too much and for the wrong reasons. Our goal is not perfection but the quiet confidence that God is bigger than our wins and losses with food.

DEALING WITH GUILT AND FAILURE

Perfectionism always has guilt and failure—its mocking cousins—close at hand. As a matter of fact, perfectionism pushes us right into their laps. When we push to be mistake-free, perfect in our quest to conquer food, defeat will certainly follow. Part of the danger in perfectionism is the unspoken goals we try to attain:

- I will never overeat.
- I will never eat something that isn't good for me.
- If I mess up, I will starve or purge my body into submission.
- Food is not to be enjoyed—it is to be mastered.

All these goals come with guilt and failure built in, because they're structured around the wrong focus. That's why diets don't bring freedom. It's also why we attach our self-worth to the grumbling stomachs of starvation or the instant relief of purging. Having the right focus is critical.

As I began to clarify my focus with food, two words kept coming to my mind: *grace* and *forgiveness*. Perfectionism began to lose its hold as I redefined my focus to sound something like this prayer:

> *Lord, I realize that the way I push my body is wrong. The unrealistic expectations I put on myself lead me to failure and guilt. Please teach me how to live in the arms of your grace. Show me how to forgive myself when I'm not perfect with food, and help me be confident that it is your healing presence leading me toward freedom. Your Word says there is no condemnation for those who are in Christ Jesus. By your strength, may I not condemn myself. In your name I pray. Amen.*

MAINTAINING A HEALTHY ATTITUDE

In his remarkable teaching, Oswald Chambers urges us to remain spiritually tenacious: "Tenacity is more than endurance—it is endurance combined with the absolute certainty that what we are looking for is going to transpire."[3]

I love this quote because, frankly, telling me to simply endure feels empty. *Tenacity* is a feisty word, filled with hope and promise. We can tenaciously know that what we're looking for—freedom from bondage and debilitating behaviors—will transpire!

I take great comfort in knowing that the Bible is filled with stories of people who didn't let their mistakes override their future blessings.

Peter was an impetuous, driven, "act-before-you–think" kind of person. Of all the people highlighted in Scripture, I relate the most to Peter. He was constantly putting his foot in his mouth, but he brought great joy to Jesus, who considered Peter as one of His best friends. Peter adored Jesus and devoted his life to knowing Him intimately. How is it, then, that within a twenty-four-hour period Peter could protectively cut the ear off a guard trying to imprison Jesus—and then turn around and deny even knowing Jesus? And it wasn't once but three times! (See Luke 22.)

Jesus restored Peter's confidence on the beach when they had breakfast together (see John 21), but I often wonder how Peter got over the guilt he felt for having denied the one he loved. Thankfully, he didn't wallow in his defeat. He let the grace of Jesus restore him to the man Jesus knew he could be and later went on to be a steadfast leader in the Early Church.

Paul is another example of tenacious faith. Can you imagine the pain Paul felt, after becoming a Christian himself from having made a living pursuing and killing Christian men and women? After a life-altering encounter with Jesus on the road to Damascus, the trajectory of Paul's life changed completely. (See Acts 9.) If Paul had stayed tied up in guilt, remorse, and condemnation because of his past actions, we wouldn't have half of the New Testament.

On a smaller scale but no less dramatic, Martha was a beacon of tenacious faith. When she became upset because her sister was dumping all the chores and responsibility onto her, she confronted Jesus with it. Jesus corrected her by bluntly saying, "Martha, Martha, you are worried and bothered about so many things; but only a few things are necessary, really only one, for Mary has chosen the good part, which shall not be taken away from her" (Luke 10:41-42).

What if Martha had marched away pouting, slamming her bedroom door to bask in bitterness after hearing these words? The truth was, Martha was trying to micromanage her family, and Jesus exposed her heart. She allowed the words and grace of Jesus to penetrate her control issues and rearrange her mind.

This tenacity is how we need to frame perfectionism in our healing with food. We recognize that we want to be obedient and free, disciplined and on-track, yet we allow ourselves the room to fail at times and then get back up and start again.

In my old way of thinking, when I overate or ate something on my "bad food" list, it triggered days, weeks, or months of bingeing and mental bashing. *I've already messed up—no point in trying to correct it!* These days, though, if I overeat at a meal, I sow seeds to the Lord the rest of the day. And the next day is a *new* day filled with promise rather than failure.

Like Peter, Paul, Martha, David, and a host of other godly brothers and sisters, I allow myself the same grace God allows me.

"Bless the Lord, O my soul, and forget none of His benefits; who pardons all your iniquities; who heals all your diseases; who redeems your life from the pit; Who crowns you with lovingkindness and compassion" (Psalm 103:2-4).

RECAPTURING YOUR SELF—IMAGE

It's not hard to see why we stray so far from a healthy self-image. From a young age, girls are inundated with unrealistic images of beauty.

As I sat in a class this past winter addressing self-image, the teacher played a one-minute video clip from YouTube. It showed a model walking into a building for a photo shoot. She was a plain-looking woman with average hair, average skin, and an average body. After the makeup artist and hair stylist finished with her, the airbrushing began. When her image reappeared, she was flawless. She had glowing skin, gorgeous hair, and a body that screamed, "10!" The short film ended by flashing to a picture of the billboard this woman now graces—unattainable perfection, for all to see and envy.

On her blog *lattesandrainydays,* Kirsten Haaland describes her journey toward understanding her body. I have her permission to share her story in its entirety with you.[4]

Dear Body,

I feel as though I owe you an apology; it is long overdue, but I'm here now, hoping that it's not too late for a little forgiveness.

Even though you are what enables me to live and to move through the world, it seems only recently that I've been especially aware of you. I've harbored nasty feelings toward you. I've abused you both verbally and physically. I've shut you up and ignored you, chained you to a pipe in the basement and padlocked the door.

I remember the first time I was shocked into an awareness of you at the age of thirteen at summer camp, when I first passed through that bloody rite of womanhood. It was a sunny morning in July. I was wearing a polka-dotted bathing suit, on my way down to the lake to go swimming, and had stopped by the restroom; that's when I noticed. I had been educated on the matter as a fifth-grader, and I knew as much about it as a thirteen-year-old could, but it still came as a terrific shock to my system. I cried and cried and cried that morning in my bunk bed, my face puffy and wet, words coming out in chokes and gasps. My counselor told me this was a beautiful gift from God, that it meant I was a woman now. But her saying that made me want to scream and rip my hair out. I didn't know why—I just hated it.

And then things really started changing: my child's body began to change shape without my willing it, malleable as Play-Doh without my consent. My straight, hipless form bloomed outward and pulled inward in places. My lithe form began to puff out, acquiring pounds that seemed to come from nowhere. I felt as though you had betrayed me. The child's body was

---

something I knew and could navigate; this new thing was foreign to me and I was trapped in it. You held me hostage.

With the added pounds came the teasing and taunts of others. I drew inward and loathed this mess of flesh I was trapped in. I was powerless to escape it, so I told you things like *You're fat and nasty. People hate you, and so do I. It would be better if you were skinnier.*

And I continued to abuse you with my words and my thoughts. I would look in the mirror and point out all your flaws, tell you to shape up, that you were no good as you were.

Finally, I had enough, and the abuse turned physical. I started memorizing food labels and adopted a plan to get you to where I thought you needed to be. *I'm in control now! I'm the boss!* I restricted calories and nutrition; I put increased physical demands on you. As the puffiness diminished and pounds evaporated, the compliments poured in, and I was addicted to them. I ate them instead of food and exercised even more, feeling proud of myself for starving you. I had taught myself to love the growling in my stomach, and I chased after that emptiness more and more.

Even when others said, "You're getting too skinny," I thought only of how to get skinnier, of how to make sure you knew that I was the one in charge here. You would not hold me hostage again. The goal was always that I'd strip you of five pounds, and when that was achieved, it would be five pounds yet again. Eventually my periods stopped, and I could pull my tiniest pair of jeans up and down, up and down while they were fully buttoned and zipped. I felt so proud. *I had tamed you.*

In college the pounds came back on slowly, and I let them return to you a few at a time, but begrudgingly. I was too worried about academics to concern myself with making sure I maintained a vigilant watch over you, to make sure you didn't get out of line. But this is where I learned new ways to push you, like staying awake when you pulled me toward sleep, ingesting cup after cup of cheap, black coffee syrupy with sugar.

I skipped meals, always reasoning that a few more minutes of study were more important than giving you those things the cafeteria attempted to pass off as food. I asked you to keep going, keep moving, keep running, and I denied you regular fuel. And then I'd get angry with you and call you names when you got sick or tired or achy or were sapped of energy. I berated you again and again, demanding health and energy and wellness even though I gave you nothing to work with.

So, my body, I'm sorry I ignored you and said unkind things. I'm sorry for having neglected and abused you. I'm sorry I've hurt you and starved you and asked impossible things of you. I'm sorry for the pain you've suffered, that we've suffered together.

We are married, you and I, and we are still learning to speak to one another; to listen with attentive ears, still learning how to move in this dance we do together. We were knit together inside my mother, and we are inseparable, you and I. My mind and heart and soul are fused with you. You are how I hug my sister, talk to my friend, how I laugh and smile. You are how I dance with joy, cry out loud, and how I can write any of this down. And so I will continue on this path of learning to be good to you: to provide what you need, not demand what you cannot give, to cooperate with you, to listen to you and respond appropriately to the things you say, to give you compassion. And I'm learning that in return you give me the ability to embody fully the life I've been given, to give my own unique shape to love, sadness, happiness, friendship, and faith.

I guess what I'm saying is that I have your back, good body of mine. We will learn this dance together, giving one another grace for the journey.

KEEPING OUR HOUSE CLEAN

As a final thought in fighting for our sanity, I would like to share a principle with you that I mentioned in an earlier chapter; the principle of keeping your house clean. I'm not talking about Windex and Mop and Glo—I'm talking about keeping your *spiritual* house clean.

In Matthew 12:43-45 Jesus explains this premise: "Now when the unclean spirit goes out of a man, it passes through waterless places, seeking rest, and does not find it. Then it says, 'I will return to my house from which I came'; and when it comes, it finds it unoccupied, swept, and put in order. Then it goes and takes along with it seven spirits more wicked than itself, and they go in and live there; and the last state of that man becomes worse than the first."

The key word in these verses is *unoccupied*. You can muster up all the self-control imaginable and feel pretty proud of your behavior for a time. But if you don't occupy your recently vacant compulsions with God's Word and proactive presence, you set yourself up for grave disappointment.

We can all sympathize with the people in the headlines who go to rehab, start making different and better choices, and for a time seem as if they're on the right track. Then, tragically, they're back in the headlines and dealing with problems that are worse than before!

Jesus is making the point that healing is serious business. It's not about quick fixes or image upkeep. It's about a lasting, daily replenishing of God's Word to us and letting His internal compass lead us away from danger.

In the book *Anointed, Transformed, Redeemed*, Priscilla Shirer shares about the potency of the awareness of God when it comes to overcoming addiction and compulsion. "Recognizing and acknowledging God's presence and perspective will alter your decisions and ultimately change outcomes."[5]

God's presence is what sustains us in knowing that we are loved and supported. We aren't left alone to figure it all out.

We can count on His promise that He will surround us with reminders that He is present.

God's perspective is what we cling to when we feel as if we're swimming upstream against the current of the world. We're choosing to live a different way and believe in the hope of God, who sings freedom over the captives.

In the spirit of keeping our houses clean, here are some thoughts to help in your daily chores.

HOUSEKEEPING CHORES FOR A CLEAN SPIRITUAL HOUSE

- Keep a healing journal handy, and write prayers to the Lord as you experience the ups and downs of temptation, victory, compulsion, and transformation.
- Pray "breath prayers" (as Richard Foster explains in his classic book titled *Prayer: Finding the Heart's True Home).* Breath prayers are phrases that can be uttered in one breath throughout the day. Some of my breath prayers sound like this:

    Thank you, Jesus, that I'm whole, free, and complete in you.

    Lord, I give this day and my choices to you.

    Help me, Jesus. Fill me, Jesus.

    You are my bread and delight, Lord.[6]
- Get outside for a walk. Nature can replenish your depleted soul.
- Sit in a coffee shop with your Bible or another good book. Sometimes just the noise and community of a coffee shop can fill you with peace.
- Share your journey with someone. Disordered eating is fueled by isolation and secrecy. Open up and let someone in.

Keeping our houses clean and occupied is a necessity that Jesus felt strongly about. What may initially feel like a chore soon becomes your new habit. Binges are replaced with prayer and fellowship. Mental bullying is replaced with breath prayers of strength and focus. Self-image is redefined to reflect God's glory. Your sanity is worth fighting for, and no one is more proud of your efforts than God himself.

Personal Morsels

Do you see yourself as a perfectionist? In what ways does this play out in your life?

_____

_____

_____

_____

_____

_____

Turn to Hebrews 10:35-36, and write it here.

_____

_____

_____

_____

_____

_____

How do these verses soothe the pain of guilt and failure?

_____

_____

_____

_____

_____

_____

How is tenacity different from endurance?

_____

_____

_____

_____

_____

_____

_____

Read Isaiah 41:9-10. How does God assure us of His presence in our battle for sanity?

_____

_____

_____

_____

_____

_____

Read Psalm 107. Which part of this psalm most clearly describes your heart?

_____

_____

_____

_____

_____

_____

A Note from the Author

Precious one,

Thank you for sharing this journey with me. I become tearful when I think of you, and the hope and belief I have for your freedom is almost uncontainable.

As one who has been through intense pain in my relationship with food, I wish I could look into your eyes and put my hands on your face. I would then tell you with all confidence that Jesus is right there with you, saying, *You will know the truth, and the truth will set you free.*

You can break the chains of lies, compulsion, sin, and heartache. This is your day! It is your time to have the life and freedom you've longed for. God is for you. He will never leave or forsake you. He is declaring new things over your life.

I am thinking of you, praying for you, and believing in you.

Until we meet in heaven,
Gari Meacham

Appendix

1. Disordered Eating Through the Eyes of Your Loved Ones

2. Raising Children to Have a Healthy Relationship with Food

3. Dieting Isn't the Answer

4. Real Stories from Real Women

Disordered Eating Through the Eyes of Your Loved Ones

In many homes, disordered eating is like a giraffe that tries to hide under an area rug. No matter how hard it tries to escape notice, its large body and intrusive presence are unavoidable. Compulsion and distorted behavior with food always leak out, and they always spill into the lives of those we love.

Although I was a master at hiding some of my worst behavior from my husband and kids, had I not received a giant U-turn call from God, the effect of my choices may have been devastating to my family.

One night shortly after I had begun to understand my issues with gluttony and compulsive dieting, I sat with my husband in a restaurant in New York City and slowly began to share with him what a mess I had become. I trembled as I shared my dark secrets with him. I was also afraid that my destructive habits with food might affect our daughter's chance of having a normal relationship with food. He listened compassionately but seemed surprised that I had struggled so.

Husbands, friends, or parents who don't struggle with food often don't seem to understand the battle you face, so their words and reactions may seem shallow and callous.

"Just eat less. How hard can it be?"

"Just eat more!"

"Join a gym and exercise!"

"Every time you eat something you shouldn't, I'm going to remind you or take it away."

Comments like these are the same as telling an injured athlete to jump over hurdles. The athlete may really want to but simply can't until he or she has healed.

Once a gentleman approached me at a writers' conference I was attending in California. He was in my critique group and had read a couple of chapters from this book. He shared his frustration with being married to a woman he deeply loved who was plagued with disordered eating. I asked him how he had penetrated his wife's heart while lies completely controlled her thinking. I also asked how he harnessed his feelings, words, and frustration when dealing with her. He told me that he's a disciplined person. His life, time, money, and appetites stay in check while his wife battles food. He said, "I just can't understand why she can't follow a few simple guidelines. Don't eat the chips out of the bag. Buy good stuff like nuts, fruits, and vegetables, and eat them when you're hungry."

He recognized that these comments were unwise and unproductive, so he learned to pray a lot and hold these comments for times when they could be received instead of rejected. He said he tried to soften some of his words with phrases such as "This will help you," "This will be best for you," "This will give you more energy," or "This will help you feel better about yourself." But after a while, he felt there was nothing new to say.

So what should husbands do? It's painful for them to watch their wives suffer as they stand idly by and shake their heads. Yet a man's help and comfort can be invaluable if he offers it in the right way. Here are some suggestions for men who want to love their wives through this time but don't know how.

- Never use sex as a tool. A friend of mine shared that her husband told her he didn't want to make love to her because of her weight. This comment has reinforced her belief that she is unlovable and undesirable, making her want to rebel with food rather than change for her husband.

- Don't put yourself in the role of food police or the one she's accountable to regarding food. When you take on that power, rather than there being a healing relationship between your spouse and the Lord, your wife will resent you and ultimately blame you for her failure.
- Encourage her spiritually with prayer, scripture, and hope. Emphasize the beauty of her spirit and the redeeming power of God to transform lives.
- Share your own struggles with her. Although you may not struggle with food, certainly there are areas of your life you want God to work on. As a ballplayer, my husband struggled with chewing tobacco. He shared with me his pain in trying to let God have this destructive habit. His authenticity encouraged me instead of pushed me away.
- Speak words of life to your wife rather than words of condemnation and guilt. Reminding your wife that she doesn't look as trim as when you married her doesn't help. She already fights voices in her head that remind her of her failures every day. Words of life and grace delight a woman's heart and encourage her to seek the healing she desperately wants.

Raising Children to Have a Healthy Relationship with Food

It takes more than carrots and apple slices to raise children to have a healthy attitude toward food. It's important to help them have a healthy mind-set and self-image as well as providing wholesome food to put in their bodies.

Time magazine recently dedicated an entire issue to the plague of obesity in America's children. They noted that "Kids are increasingly sedentary, spending three hours a day in front of a TV or computer. Physical education is vanishing too, with only 25 percent of kids attending."[1]

Suburban children's activities are usually arranged for them. Sports, dance, gymnastics, and karate all keep Mom's taxi on the road and her schedule full. Many children, though, don't have these opportunities, because either they aren't available where they live, or their parents don't have the time or the money for them to participate. It's been found that in 10- to 17-year-olds who live below the poverty line, 22.4 percent are overweight or obese. In families whose income is four times that level or higher, the overweight or obesity rate of the children is just 9.1 percent.[2] Because junk food and processed food is cheaper than the more nutritious fruits, vegetables, and meats, many families who struggle financially opt for the low-cost items. Even if they would like to provide better food for the children, they simply can't afford it.

On the flipside, those of us who have struggled with restricted eating and diets have unknowingly preached silent sermons to our watchful children. Children internalize parents' struggles with food when the parents complain about being overweight, restrict everything they eat, or continually criticize themselves for their eating patterns. This usually causes parents to turn a critical eye to what the children eat, because they don't want the children to end up with the same sorts of problems with food that they've experienced themselves.

I've heard of children as young as six being put on a diet by their parents. Convinced that they're doing something healthful for their children, these parents don't realize that the most important action they can take in shaping their children's future with food is modeling health and freedom themselves. I often tell women that the most effective thing they can do for their families is to focus all their energy and attention on their own personal healing with food. This ensuing peace and assurance invite the children to choose not to adopt their parents' former eating rituals and dark belief system regarding food.

My older daughter was three when a babysitter told me "I've never seen a child who could eat so much food and not get sick!" I panicked.

Immediately I thought of my own failures and how I had probably damaged her already. As I prayerfully took my fear to God, I realized that I had a lot of wisdom to share with my daughter as she grew.

One strategy I employed immediately was what our family nicknamed "tummy talk." I would ask the kids, "What does your tummy say?" when they wanted second helpings or more of something. This question allowed them to think for themselves and learn to gage their own hunger scale. I never tried to correct their assessment of their tummy talk. If they said, "My tummy says I can have more," I encouraged them to take a small second helping and ask themselves again what their tummy said. Often they would reply, "My tummy says it's full," and they would walk away from eating past the point of fullness.

This strategy offered daily practice in learning how to listen to their hungry/full gage, and it took me out of the role of deciding how much food they should eat and when to eat it.

For some parents, the battle is trying to get their young children to eat. They coax, bribe, punish, and beg their kids to eat against their will. I've seen children refuse to eat simply because they wanted the upper hand in their struggle with their parents. Some children aren't really hungry at the traditional morning, noon, or evening times we've designated for meals. Our family remedied this by having the children sit with us at the meal. If they weren't hungry, they didn't have to eat, but it was understood that when they were hungry, they ate leftovers of what we had, not junk or snack food.

Children are born with perfect hunger responses, and we should continue to encourage those throughout childhood. As kids get older, the influence of peers and the cultural pull of television and movies starts to mold their self-images. "Children are developing body dissatisfaction and body image concerns at younger ages," comments Jennifer Hagman, director of the eating disorders program at The Children's Hospital in Denver. She gives this advice to parents:

- If children mention weight concerns, let them know that changes in body shape are normal, especially during puberty.
- Watch what you say. Making disparaging statements about food, weight, body size, or body shape can put your child on a lifelong path of negative thinking.
- Let your kids participate in decisions about what to eat, but be sure healthful choices are available.
- Compliment your child on things unrelated to physical appearance, such as efforts in school, athleticism, or other special talents.

- Restrict television viewing or join your children in watching their favorite shows so you can put images into perspective.
- Listen to your children. The more you understand about your children's lives and concerns, the more you can help establish a healthy foundation for adulthood.[3]

Dieting Isn't the Answer

As we know for ourselves, dieting doesn't work. So why would we think it works for our children? Alison Field of Children's Hospital Boston has been following the weight-control behaviors of almost 17,000 kids and agrees with diet backlash. "We actually find that children who diet gain more weight than their peers. It's not just that kids who diet tend to gain back the weight later; it's that dieting brings up all sorts of unbidden psychological responses that sabotage the process. After all, self-deprivation is one thing; being told by someone else that you can't eat—even when you feel hungry—is another."[4]

It's invaluable for parents to model eating as a response to hunger and stopping when full. Honoring our children's effort at this, and working on this as a family, is a powerful step toward a healthy relationship with food.

Another important issue to consider when raising children to form healthy habits is how we use our words. In my classroom I had a poster that stated, "Sticks and stones may break my bones, but words will break my heart." This is in sharp contrast to the chant we recited as kids "—but words will never hurt me." Words *do* hurt, and how we respond to children matters.

Teach children to be in control, but set limits. By offering choices of a variety of good foods and letting children select what they want, you empower their belief that they can be in control while still feeling protected by you. Be careful with your language as it pertains to your children's eating habits. You don't want them to think of you as the food police.

"Don't eat that. It'll make you fat!"

"The other children can have a cookie, but you need a carrot."

"You're allowed only foods that have no sugar, fat, or artificial ingredients. These are your choices."

"Don't you want to be skinny like your friends?"

If you're accustomed to badgering your children with controlling words or actions, ask God to give you new messages to relay to them—messages of hope, faith, and encouragement. This can be your seed-sowing—dedicated to the health and sanity of your children.

Real Stories from Real Women

I was a dancer and model at a young age, constantly exposed to the entertainment world, where, as they say, "Image is everything." Appearance is crucial, and being thin is expected. It's nearly impossible not to obsess about looks.

Growing up, I was always extremely skinny, and it makes me laugh now thinking of all the times I used to pray I would gain some weight and not look so gangly! It wasn't until college, when I was working as a professional dancer, that the days of eating whatever I wanted finally caught up with me. Between working as a Los Angeles Laker Girl, going on tour with a music artist, and taking all my dance major classes, I spent most of every entire day staring at my body in the mirror. I learned to pick out my flaws and scrutinize each area of my body that wasn't "good enough." I knew if I gained weight, it wasn't because I didn't get enough exercise—it was all about food. I confessed that I was a compulsive eater.

Through Truly Fed I was able to learn I could redefine and recreate who I am with food. I could be satisfied after eating—not stuffed, bloated, and guilty. I could stop bingeing on junk food—or sometimes even healthful food—and using the excuse that I would burn it off later in dance class.

One of the profound concepts of Truly Fed that resonates with me is the idea of sowing seeds. My sowing helped me stop eating the second I start to feel full and battling the lies Satan tells me about my body.

I created a vision of a day when I wouldn't even think about what I was going to eat for breakfast, lunch, or dinner and wasn't going to compare myself to every girl who walked by or was on my team. I wasn't going to pinch at the fat on my thighs anymore.

I'm so happy to say that the vision is now reality. I feel as I did as a child, eating whatever I wanted with no regret! *Truly Fed* is a book not just about food—it's a book about freedom, deliverance, and the confidence that only Jesus can provide.

—*Ally Meacham Evans*

A huge moment of awareness happened as I read *Truly Fed* and came to recognize my fear of anger. It was blocking my freedom in other disciplines. I realized that it's all about letting God in and praising Him no matter what's happening. I learned not to think "weight loss" but to focus on freedom—not freedom to do whatever I want but the freedom to be obedient to God. I understand now that whatever I sow to God will reap peace and wisdom. The world tries to change me from the outside in through diets and fads, but God can change me from the inside out. I still have habits I work on and surrender to Him daily, but I'm free to eat in moderation. I'm free to accept my over-60 body as it changes with the aging process. I'm free to envision the self God wants for me—emotionally and spiritually healthy as well as physically healthy.

—*Bev Saylor*

I fought my weight my whole life. I can remember as far back as kindergarten and crying because I got a new swimsuit and it was too small. In junior high I took control and lost weight but regained weight in college. I lost more and gained some. I was never free. I always wanted to weigh less. I never had a clinical eating disorder with a name, but I had a social eating disorder, the need to be thin as defined by society rather than by God. Now I want to be thin because God intended my body to be a temple—not a trough where I keep storing more and more food.

I feel I've been set free from counting calories—something I was resigned to doing for the rest of my life. I've taken the scale out of the bedroom and put it in the basement. I don't even remember to weigh myself. Now that's freedom! I'm finished with the good food/bad food list.

During the first few weeks of Truly Fed I lost five pounds without doing anything except working to change my diet attitude to God-focused attitude. He's the one I want to please, not the world. He's the one I want to avoid sinning against, not the ideas of how I want to look in my head. He's the offering of forgiveness, not the scale. He's in control, not me.

I spent time journaling about my weight. I sowed seeds. I told people about my freedom. Without the daily connection to God, I would be lost. Through this study I'm free from being controlled by food. It took Truly Fed to help me give God access to this part of my life.

—*Cindy Yallop*

I've struggled with both restricting and bulimia, so I must guard against allowing sowing seeds to become a form of self-punishment. I think this is really a matter of the position of my heart. One of my favorite moments of sowing seeds came on a trip to Costco. I needed to run in and grab a few items over my lunch hour, and I hadn't yet eaten the lunch I brought to work that day. I was a little hungry, and I knew I was walking into a field of temptation with all the sample stands. I mentally prepared myself to sow seeds as I traveled by these samplers. Each stand I passed called to me, and I fought hard to stay away. Gradually I got a little closer to the food, just for a look. At the next stand I said, "Well, I can have just one." As I put the item in my hand, it crumbled, and I was forced to throw it away. Knowing that this happened for a reason, I laughed at my stubbornness and kept walking. I said to myself in a firm yet loving voice, *This is not restricting—this is worship!* I said it over and over as I walked through the store. "This is worship. This is worship. This is worship."

If I tell myself I can't have something because it's *bad* or because I'm depriving myself of it, I'll only eat it more. Sowing seeds needs to be bigger than restricting certain foods or not eating through certain times of the day. It's a time to worship. It's a time to die to myself and my desires.

Sowing seeds for me has also been choosing not to purge if I've binged. I know that neither bingeing nor purging is good for my body or my spirit. I know that purging perpetuates the cycle of disorder—and stopping that cycle by sowing the desire to rid my body of the food I've consumed honors God. After a binge I feel miserable, and often the desire to rid my body of the food has little to do with fear of weight gain but more a desire to undo what I've done. Forcing myself to live with the consequences of my actions and be accountable for my behavior is part of my maturing process. A good friend once said that maturing is not getting old—it's growing up, literally. Upward to God!

—*Tracy Tchamanzar*

NOTES

Chapter 1

1. Stephen Arterburn, *Healing Is a Choice* (Nashville: Thomas Nelson, 2005), xix.

2. William Barclay, *The Gospel of John, Vol. 1* (Louisville, Ky.: Westminster John Knox Press, 1975), 179-80.

3. Brennan Manning, *The Importance of Being Foolish* (New York: Harper Collins, 2005), 5-10. Used by permission.

4. Oswald Chambers, *My Utmost for His Highest*, Classic Edition (Grand Rapids: Barbour, 1963), 47.

5. *Merriam-Webster's Collegiate Dictionary*, 11th ed., s.v. "save."

6. Joanna Weaver, *Having a Mary Heart in a Martha World* (Colorado Springs: WaterBrook Press, 2000), 105-7.

7. Quoted in Sue Monk Kidd, *Firstlight* (New York: Penguin, 2007), 17-18.

Chapter 2

1. Diane Hampton, *The Diet Alternative* (New Kensington, Pa.: Whitaker House, 1984).

2. *Merriam-Webster's Collegiate Dictionary*, 11th ed., s.v. "gluttony."

3. Hampton, *The Diet Alternative*, 10-11.

4. Chambers, *My Utmost for His Highest*, 281.

5. Weaver, *Having a Mary Heart in a Martha World*, 111.

6. Geneen Roth, "Confessions of a Food Sneak," *Prevention*, February 2006, 88.

7. Eugene H. Peterson, *The Message* (Colorado Springs: NavPress, 2002), 2236.

8. Beth Moore, *Stepping Up: A Journey Through the Psalms of Ascent* (Nashville: LifeWay Press, 2007), 81.

Chapter 3

1. Geneen Roth, *Breaking Free from Compulsive Eating* (New York: NAL Penguin, 1986), 5.

2. Shirley Billigmeier, *Inner Eating* (Nashville: Thomas Nelson, 1991), 50.

3. Bob Greene, "Best Life Diet: The Basics," <http://www.oprah.com/article/health/weightloss/basics.scale>, August 4, 2008.

4. Wendy Oliver Pratt, M.D., *Fed Up* (New York: McGraw-Hill, 2003), 21.

Chapter 4
1. Hampton, *The Diet Alternative*, 98.

Chapter 5
1. Arterburn, *Healing Is a Choice*, 125.

2. John Eldredge, *Wild at Heart* (Nashville: Thomas Nelson, 2001), 106.

3. Larry Crabb spoke at a gathering of Professional Baseball Wives at Coors Field, Denver, in the late 1990s.

4. Hampton, *The Diet Alternative*, 129.

5. Chambers, *My Utmost for His Highest*, 74.

Chapter 6
1. Quoted on One Way Jesus website, <http://www.godwyn.blogspot.com>

2. Charles Stanley, *When the Enemy Strikes* (Nashville: Thomas Nelson Ppublishers, 2004), 116.

3. Pratt, *Fed Up*, 27.

4. Ibid., 28.

5. Tim Hansel, *Holy Sweat* (Waco, Tex.: Word, 1987) 102-3.

6. Weaver, *Having a Mary Heart in a Martha World*, 119.

Chapter 7
1. Old greeting card, <http://www.eons.com/blogs/entry/358336-He-Was-Only-A-Chocolate-Chip-Cookie>.

2. Jan Johnson, *When Food Is Your Best Friend and Worst Enemy* (New York: Harper Collins, 1993), 24.

3. Overeaters Anonymous, "In Answer to Your Inquiry," an OA brochure (Torrance, Calif.: Overeaters Anonymous, 1982), middle inside page.

4. Johnson, *When Food Is Your Best Friend*, 27.

5. Jennifer Rothchild, *Fingerprints of God* (Nashville: LifeWay Press, 2005), 68.

6. Quoted in Emily Yoffe, "But I Don't Eat That Much," O, *The Oprah Magazine*, February 2007, 102.

7. Mark Batterson, *In a Pit with a Lion on a Snowy Day* (Sisters, Oreg.: Multnomah Publishers, 2006), 136.

Chapter 8
1. Statistics from the National Eating Disorders Association, <http://www.edap.org./p.asp?WebPage_ID=320& Profile_ID=41138>, June 2007.

2. Quoted in Joan Webb, *The Relief of Imperfection* (Ventura, Calif.: Regal, 2007), 117.

3. Chambers, *My Utmost for His Highest*, 53.

4. Taken from the blog site *lattesandrainydays* and written by Kirsten Haaland.

5. Priscilla Shirer, *Anointed, Transformed, Redeemed* (Nashville: Life-Way Press, 2008), 18.

6. Richard Foster, *Prayer: Finding the Heart's True Home* (New York: HarperCollins, 1992), 122-24.

Appendix

1. Jeffrey Kluger, "How American Children Packed On the Pounds," *Time*, June 23, 2008, 66.

2. Bryan Walsh, "It's Not Just Genetics," *Time*, June 23, 2008, 78.

3. Beth Tomkiw, "Eye of the Beholder," *Vim and Vigor*, fall 2007, 46.

4. Lori Oliwenstein, "Weighty Issues," *Time*, June 23, 2008, 102.

YOU DON'T HAVE TO LIVE WITH A POOR SELF-IMAGE.

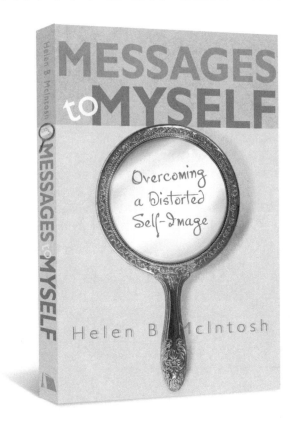

This helpful, inspirational book shows you how to see yourself as God sees you and live in peace and joy with eager anticipation for your future. Dr. Helen McIntosh, a licensed counselor, has experienced the emotional anguish and devastation that past hurts can cause. In *Messages to Myself*, she shares with you the methods that you can start using immediately to change the messages you give yourself every day.

Do you long to fall in love with God?

In this inspiring and relevant book, Debra White Smith shows you how to satisfy your nagging hunger for the fullness of God's love. Through the author's helpful insights and solid biblical wisdom, you will begin the journey of a deepening romance with the Lord that will bring you ever nearer to the heart of God.

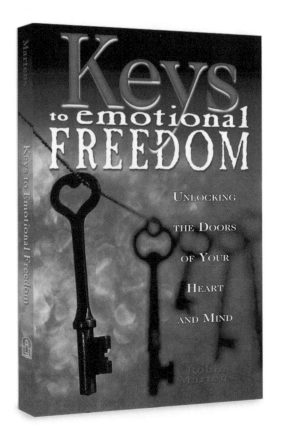